RETURN ON REAL ESTATE

RETURN ON REAL ESTATE

Creative Strategies to **Cash Out** or **Cash Flow**

LEKA DEVATHA

BiggerPockets PUBLISHING
Denver, Colorado

Praise for *Return on Real Estate*

"*Return on Real Estate* delivers the kind of real-world strategies that even experienced investors can appreciate. Leka's transparency, creativity, and resourcefulness make this a must-read for anyone looking to maximize their options—whether you're building long-term cash flow or positioning for a big exit."

> —**Devon Kennard**, former NFL Linebacker, Private Lender, and author of *Real Estate Side Hustle*

"*Return on Real Estate* isn't just another investing book—it's a behind-the-scenes look at what it really takes to build a portfolio when money is tight and markets are tough. What I love most is how honest and practical it is. The author doesn't just share wins; she walks you through the messy pivots, creative exits, and lessons earned the hard way. Whether you're just getting started or looking to scale smartly, this book will give you real strategies you can actually use. Highly recommend."

> —**Ashley Kehr**, cohost of the BiggerPockets *Real Estate Rookie* podcast, author of *Real Estate Rookie* and coauthor of *Real Estate Partnerships*

"*Return on Real Estate* is the book we wish more of our clients would read before jumping into a deal. Leka doesn't just teach strategy; she shows readers how to build lasting wealth with clarity, creativity, and confidence. From calculating ROI and 1031 exchanges, to ADUs to property exits, her guidance is tactical and filled with real-world examples that are super relatable. Whether you're on your first flip or scaling a multimillion-dollar portfolio, this book bridges the gap between numbers and mindset, making it a must-read for new and experienced investors alike."

> —**Amanda Han & Matt MacFarland**, CPAs, authors of the *Tax Strategies* series

"An incredible resource with actionable insights that every investor can employ. Don't miss your chance to learn from Leka—she's one of the best investors and educators in the business."

—**Dave Meyer**, host of the *BiggerPockets Real Estate* podcast, author of *Start with Strategy*

"Leka totally crushed it with *Return on Real Estate*! She breaks down game-changing strategies—from flipping and subdivisions to ADUs and assisted living—that'll help you maximize cash flow and cash out BIG, even in expensive markets. This book isn't theory; it's full of real-life, actionable stories about scaling your portfolio creatively without needing piles of cash to start. Seriously, if you're ready to level up your real estate investing, stop what you're doing and grab this book NOW!"

—**Tony Robinson**, cohost of the BiggerPockets *Real Estate Rookie* podcast, coauthor of *Real Estate Partnerships*

"*Return on Real Estate* is honest, tactical, and grounded in real-world experience—a clear and practical guide for investors who want to succeed."

—**James Dainard**, expert flipper of "Million Dollar Zombie Flips," author of *The House Flipping Framework*

Return on Real Estate: Creative Strategies to Cash Out or Cash Flow
Leka Devatha

Published by BiggerPockets Publishing LLC, Denver, CO
Copyright © 2025 by Leka Devatha
All rights reserved.

Publisher's Cataloging-in-Publication Data
Names: Devatha, Leka, author.
Title: Return on real estate : creative strategies to cash out or cash flow / Leka Devatha.
Description: Denver, CO: BiggerPockets Publishing LLC, 2025.
Identifiers: LCCN: 2025938135 | ISBN: 9781960178794 (paperback) | 9781960178800 (ebook)
Subjects: LCSH Real estate investment. | Real estate investment--Finance. | Real estate business. | Cash
flow. | Personal finance. | Investments. | BISAC BUSINESS & ECONOMICS / Real Estate / Buying & Selling
Homes | BUSINESS & ECONOMICS / Investments & Securities / Real Estate | BUSINESS & ECONOMICS /
Personal Finance / Investing
Classification: LCC HD1382.5 .D49 2025 | DDC 332.63/24--dc23

Published in the United States of America
10 9 8 7 6 5 4 3 2 1

To all the fearless entrepreneurs, savvy investors, and determined individuals who dare to dream big and work tirelessly to turn their passions into profits.

May this book be your trusted guide, empowering you to navigate the world of real estate investing with confidence, creativity, and unwavering perseverance.

To my family, friends, and mentors who have supported me every step of the way, I offer my deepest gratitude.

And to those who are just starting their journey, I dedicate this book to you—may it inspire, educate, and motivate you to achieve greatness.

Always remember, success is not just about achieving your goals, but about the person you become in the process.
—My mother

Table of Contents

Introduction

Growing up in India was a kaleidoscopic experience, filled with vibrant colors, diverse traditions, and endless love. I was part of a sprawling family that included my incredible parents, two siblings, and a staggering twenty-seven first cousins. Our home was a bustling hub, where eleven family members and fourteen boisterous dogs lived together under one roof.

For those who wonder if the concept of joint families in India is real, I'm living proof that it's not just a stereotype—it's a beautiful, chaotic reality!

School was the cornerstone of my childhood in India, where academic excellence is deeply ingrained in the culture. As a child, academics reigned supreme. While extracurricular activities like sports and arts were encouraged, they were secondary to our grades.

I threw myself into my studies, and fortunately, my hard work paid off. The pressure to perform was relentless, but it drove me to succeed. Looking back, I realize that these experiences shaped me in ways that go beyond academics.

My parents took divergent approaches to raising my siblings and me. My dad, a traditional Indian patriarch, was fiercely protective, especially when it came to my sister and me. In contrast, my mom was a progressive force, encouraging us to be independent, fearless, and self-sufficient. I feel fortunate to have had two supportive role models who not only provided love and care but also instilled valuable life lessons.

In my childhood, I was surrounded by a culture that deeply respected tradition and authority. Questioning the status quo wasn't encouraged, and entrepreneurship was seen as a rare and unconventional career path. However, my dad defied these conventions. He was a true pioneer, with a passion for innovation and a drive to succeed.

As a serial entrepreneur, my dad had an infectious energy that led him to launch company after company. He was always chasing new ideas and opportunities, and his enthusiasm was inspiring. His entrepreneurial ventures took him far beyond his successful restaurant business, which served traditional Indian dishes that were beloved by our local community.

I remember watching my dad work tirelessly, juggling multiple projects and pursuing his passions with unwavering dedication. His work ethic was impressive, and his ability to adapt and evolve in the face of challenges was truly inspiring. As I grew older, I began to realize the impact my dad's entrepreneurial spirit had on our family and community.

His ventures created jobs, stimulated local economic growth, and brought people together. My dad's success was not just about personal achievement; it was about making a positive difference in the world. As I reflect on my own entrepreneurial journey, I am grateful for the lessons I learned from my dad. His legacy continues to inspire me to pursue my passions, take calculated risks, and strive for excellence in all that I do.

Even though his business in the food industry was thriving, my dad kept a keen eye out for other opportunities. He often shared his insights with me, and one conversation in particular has stayed with me. During my high school years, he offered me a piece of advice that seemed simple yet profound: "If you have just one dollar, invest it in land." He firmly believed that land was a finite resource, and I've come to share his conviction.

Looking back, I wonder if my dad had a glimpse of my future, one that I couldn't see yet. Did he know that I would eventually find my passion in real estate? His words of wisdom planted a seed in my mind, and years later, I would harvest the fruits of his advice.

A Spark

In the summer of 2001, I was an 18-year-old living in India, and I desperately wanted to attend a Bryan Adams concert. It was a rare opportunity, as logistical and legal hurdles often prevented U.S. artists from performing in India. But Bryan was coming, and I was determined to be there.

Defying my parents' wishes, I snuck out to the concert. It was nothing short of incredible. But, as it often does, consequence caught up with me.

My reward for rebellion? A month-long grounding. My social life was put on ice, with college classes being my only escape. Weekdays blurred together, but weekends felt like an eternity.

Just when I thought I'd lose my mind, my mother took pity on me. She granted me a temporary reprieve, allowing me to attend a crafting workshop. It may not sound thrilling, but to an 18-year-old stuck in solitary confinement, it was a lifeline.

The workshop was a surprise hit. I discovered a hidden talent for molding bread dough into picture frames and gift baskets. It was an unconventional art form, but I was hooked. As I honed my skills, a business idea began to rise, much like a perfectly proofed loaf.

What started as a creative escape from punishment turned out to be something much bigger. As I shaped and glazed those whimsical bread creations, something clicked. For the first time, I realized I could make things with my hands—and make money doing it. I wasn't just crafting; I was creating value. That moment was my first glimpse into what it meant to be an entrepreneur. Rebellion had landed me in that workshop, but revelation would launch me out of it—with a business in hand and a spark that would never go out.

Before I knew it, BreadCraft was born. I turned my passion into a company and took the leap, opening a retail store. Who would have thought that a crafting workshop would be the catalyst for a successful entrepreneurial venture?

And so, my entrepreneurial journey began at just 18 years old. I'd be remiss not to give a nod to Bryan Adams, whose concert sparked the chain of events, and my mom, who inadvertently fueled my entrepreneurial fire.

Pioneering New Paths

I firmly believe that immigrating to a new country is the ultimate test of personal development, much like climbing Mount Everest is the pinnacle of adventure and exploration. Both feats demand extraordinary grit, perseverance, and a clear vision.

Just as scaling the world's highest peak pushes you to your physical and mental limits, immigration challenges your entire being. It forces you to adapt, to innovate, and to evolve. You must navigate unfamiliar landscapes, forge new connections, and rebuild your sense of identity. It's a journey that requires unrelenting determination, resilience, and hope.

At 24 years old, I met the love of my life: a brilliant software engineer at Microsoft, living in Seattle. For six enchanting months, we bridged the distance between us, our hearts beating as one despite the ocean between us. We poured our souls into emails and Skype calls, sharing every detail of our lives.

Then the moment of truth arrived. We met in person, and the connection was undeniable. Within a whirlwind week, we knew we were meant to be. With hearts full of joy and excitement, we decided to take the leap and get married! I bid farewell to India, leaving behind the familiar comforts of home. The faces I grew up with, the flavors that danced on my tongue, the streets I wandered—everything I knew and loved would now be 7,000 miles away.

As I stepped into my new life, every sense was heightened. The crisp air was different, the fashion was bold, the currency was unfamiliar, and the food was a culinary adventure. Even with English as my primary language, colloquialisms and slang left me bewildered. I felt like Alice tumbling down the rabbit hole, entering a fantastical world that was both thrilling and terrifying.

As the months passed in Seattle, I made a startling realization: I had left behind more than just familiar faces and flavors. I had also left behind my entrepreneurial spark. The same fire that had driven me to turn a simple glazed bread into a profitable venture as an 18-year-old now seemed like a distant memory.

As I struggled to adjust to my new life, I found myself drained of the energy and creativity needed to blaze a new business trail. Instead, I joined the ranks of many spouses of immigrant visa holders, desperate to find any job at any company that would hire me. It was a humbling experience, one that tested my resilience and forced me to reevaluate my priorities.

My professional journey in the United States began at Nordstrom, where I started as a sales associate on the floor. My time at the renowned department store was filled with growth—I climbed the ladder from sales floor to corporate headquarters, and even welcomed a precious baby during that season. But as fulfilling as it looked on paper, I couldn't shake the feeling that I was meant for something more.

I missed building things from scratch. I missed the creativity, the adrenaline, and the ownership I had felt while running BreadCraft. I didn't want to just do a job—I wanted more. I just didn't know more of *what* yet.

Then one afternoon, everything changed. I was driving during my lunch break when a thirty-second radio ad for a house flipping workshop stopped me in my tracks. I pulled over and replayed the words in my head. Could this be the spark I'd been searching for?

I signed up. I showed up. And in just one hour, my entire view of real estate—and my future—shifted.

Although I could only spare an hour during my lunch break, that single hour at the workshop was life changing. For the first time, I grasped the astonishing reality that anyone could own multiple properties. I was captivated by the concepts of passive income, rental properties, and house flipping. The speaker's words—"sales," "deals," "portfolio growth"—were like a foreign language, but I was desperate to learn. I hung onto every syllable, absorbing it like a sponge. And when I returned to work, my mind was racing with possibilities.

The next six months were filled with intense learning. I devoured books, enrolled in a comprehensive course, and sought guidance from industry experts who generously shared their time and expertise. I mastered deal analysis, learned the art of raising private capital, and expanded my network by attending local real estate events. With unwavering dedication, I was an A-plus student and took advantage of every learning opportunity.

At one of the real estate events, fate brought me together with an old friend from my Nordstrom days. He had transitioned into a new role as an escrow officer and had connections in the industry. Through him, I met an investor who was actively flipping houses, and that introduction led to another valuable connection: a seasoned wholesaler.

A wholesaler plays a pivotal role as a middleman in the real estate industry. Their strategy involves identifying undervalued or distressed properties, securing them under contract, and then assigning that contract to an investor. The investor, often with a renovation plan in place, can then unlock the property's true value, while the wholesaler earns a profit from the assignment of the contract.

Through this wholesaler, I secured my very first real estate deal. It was a charming single-family home (SFH) in a picturesque Seattle suburb. This pivotal moment marked the official launch of my real estate journey, and there was no looking back.

Today, I've had the privilege of leading hundreds of transactions, spanning renovations, listings, wholesale deals, and beyond. I've shared my expertise on numerous podcasts and media channels, and I'm proud to host one of Seattle's most popular real estate events. Perhaps most notably, I've raised over $30 million in private capital.

You may be wondering why I've shared my story with you. The reason is simple: I want to inspire you to believe in your own potential. If a young girl from India can navigate unfamiliar cultural and real estate landscapes to achieve financial freedom, joy, community, and resilience, then I have no doubt that you can too.

My journey has been a wild adventure, but it's shown me that the destination is achievable, and the journey is worth it. On the days when the road ahead seems uncertain, I want you to draw upon my story and remind yourself: *I can do this.* Repeat it often, especially when the journey gets tough. Trust me, it's worth it.

My journey wasn't a coincidence; it was a deliberate choice. What I love about real estate investing is that there's no road map. Instead, you have the freedom to forge your own path, to choose your own adventure, and to create the success you envision.

Ready, Set, Invest! Let the Real Estate Adventure Begin!

This book might be your first step into a real estate adventure—or it might be your 247th. Either way, after you read this book, I want you to be inspired to take action. Most of the time, people simply lack ideas. It's not a lack of desire, motivation, or stick-to-it mindset that's the problem; it's that they don't know what to do next. I hope that my book is an idea-generating machine full of aha moments for both new and seasoned investors. Whether you are embarking on this adventure lacking the capital, the time, or the network necessary to succeed, it is my sincerest wish and goal that this book will show you how to create each of those in an easy-to-follow way. All you need to do is choose your path.

If I've learned anything in my decade of investing, it's to expect the unexpected. There are dozens of different paths you can take and countless obstacles you may have to face. Hopefully, armed with the knowledge in this book, you'll be able to tackle this adventure with confidence and achieve your goals.

PART 1

Understanding Your Return

What to Expect

If you are a seasoned investor looking to level up your game . . .

If you are looking to make a career pivot or a change the way in which you do business in the real estate world . . .

If you are looking to leave your nine-to-five job . . .

If you are hearing the call to change course and discover a new career entirely . . .

If you are looking for a path to financial freedom . . .

If you are hoping to find a way to increase your wealth using the foundational network you've already built . . .

If you want to build a portfolio of more than just properties, but instead a legacy . . .

This book is for you.

And if you are a brand-new investor, there is a fire hose of information for you in this book. I'll try to keep the flow manageable, but hold on to your hat, because this is going to be a wild ride!

The stories and experiences in this book span over a decade of my life spent investing in a variety of market landscapes. My journey has been unconventional. It hasn't been problem free, but despite the odds and obstacles, I've found a way to be successful. As I write this book, I have completed over a hundred full-gut renovations and own a sizable portfolio of properties.

I have renovated and sold distressed properties in a very hot market and also navigated a market completely devoid of inventory. I have worked in a market that is so sizzling hot that offers land on each property's doorstep one after another after another, as well as in a market in which buyers frustratingly fade into the mist thanks to sudden and severe rises in interest rates. In the past ten years, I have seen so much, and I have learned so much. By sharing my experiences, I want to help you both avoid repeating my mistakes and find ways to imitate my successes.

In this book, we will cover some of my most iconic discoveries about buying and stabilizing distressed properties. We will talk about the ultimate return on investment (ROI), whether it's dealing with properties, your network, or your capital. You will also learn about creative ways to structure your deals, expandability (how to force massive returns by identifying what is possible), and how to tackle adversity.

In this book, we will specifically cover:

- Evaluating returns in real estate.
- Different exit strategies in real estate.
- Equity-based strategies to boost ROI.
- Value-add strategies to boost ROI.
- Why, when, and how to sell your property.
- And more!

Launching Your Real Estate Adventure

Remember those thrilling *Choose Your Own Adventure* books from childhood? Where you stepped into the story and made choices that shaped the outcome?

Now, imagine that same excitement and agency but with higher stakes and greater rewards. Welcome to the ultimate interactive guide to real estate investing!

In this immersive journey, you'll navigate the world of real estate, making pivotal decisions that impact your financial growth and personal fulfillment. Every choice you make propels you forward, presenting opportunities for triumph or lessons from setbacks.

Select a character that mirrors your aspirations and follow their lead through a series of real-world scenarios. Each chapter presents critical decisions that will direct your journey toward success. This isn't just a book; it's a tool kit. And you're not going it alone. You'll learn alongside five investor profiles, each one with their own goals, challenges, and victories.

Get ready to:

- Make impactful choices that drive your financial growth.
- Seize opportunities and transform challenges into triumphs.
- Develop a deeper understanding of real estate investing strategies.
- Unlock your potential for success and personal fulfillment.

"The future belongs to those who believe in the beauty of their dreams." —Eleanor Roosevelt

MEET NEW-TO-THE-GAME NOAH

Hi, I'm Noah! I'm excited to embark on my real estate journey, driven by a passion to escape the nine-to-five grind and build my own wealth. With no prior experience, I'm relying on determination and a willingness to learn.

I'm on the hunt for valuable mentorship, effective strategies, and a clear road map to success. My goals are straightforward.

- Build steady cash flow
- Gain momentum in the market
- Avoid costly rookie mistakes

While I'm a bit nervous, I'm ready to dive in, learn from every step, and turn my dreams into reality.

MEET ACTIVE ALEX

Hi, I'm Alex! I'm a DIY enthusiast with a passion for transforming properties with my own two hands. With a trusty toolbox by my side, I'm always ready to roll up my sleeves and tackle the next challenge.

As a self-motivated problem-solver, I thrive on hard work and getting things done. My goal is to achieve financial freedom and control over my investments, and I'm willing to put in the effort to make it happen.

I'm a firm believer in the value of hands-on experience and attention to detail. Whether it's a major renovation or a simple fix, I prefer to take on the task myself, ensuring that every aspect meets my high standards. With a focus on quality and a willingness to learn, I'm ready to dive deep into the world of real estate and make my mark.

MEET PIVOT PEYTON

Hi, I'm Peyton! I'm a free-thinking, adaptable, and creative force to be reckoned with in the world of real estate. I thrive on change and innovation, always seeking out the best deals and cutting-edge strategies to maximize my properties' potential and achieve financial freedom.

As a trend-savvy investor, I stay ahead of the curve, constantly monitoring market shifts and adjusting my approach to capitalize on new opportunities. I'm not afraid to take calculated risks and experiment with novel approaches to ensure my portfolio remains vibrant and profitable.

With a passion for pushing boundaries and a willingness to challenge conventional wisdom, I'm always in the driver's seat, navigating the ever-changing landscape of real estate and shaping my own success.

MEET SEASONED-INVESTOR SAM

Hello, everyone, I'm Sam, a seasoned investor with a rich history in the real estate world. With a diverse portfolio and an extensive network of industry connections, I've established a strong foundation for success.

Now I'm driven by a desire to leave a lasting legacy and take my investments to new heights. I'm not content with simply maintaining the status quo; I'm eager to grow, evolve, and elevate my real estate game. I'm willing to take calculated risks that promise substantial returns, and my current focus is on securing more lucrative deals that will propel me forward.

MEET LONG-GAME LOGAN

Hi, I'm Logan. As a veteran investor, I've shifted my focus from chasing short-term gains to prioritizing long-term stability and results.

With strategic thinking and delegation as my strongest skills, I've mastered the art of efficient investing. I value time freedom, peace of mind, and a balanced lifestyle over the daily grind of active management. My goal is to reap the rewards of my past efforts, enjoying passive income without the hassle.

I'm a firm believer in working smarter, not harder. By leveraging my experience and investing strategically, I've created a portfolio that generates returns without requiring my constant involvement. I'm living proof that with the right approach, real estate investing can be a key to unlocking a life of freedom and financial security.

Unlock the Power of Vicarious Learning

Embracing a new way of learning can feel unconventional, but it's precisely this approach that can accelerate your growth exponentially. By learning through the experiences of others, you can sidestep costly mistakes and gain invaluable insights.

That's likely why you're reading this book: to tap into the knowledge of a seasoned real estate investor. Now, take it a step further by immersing yourself in the persona of your chosen character, the one who resonates most with your goals and aspirations.

Rather than overwhelming yourself with a deluge of information, focus on the specific insights that matter most to you. Each character's unique motivations and goals will guide you in understanding the different aspects of real estate investing.

For instance, when evaluating investment performance, each character's priorities will lead them to favor specific metrics over others. By learning through their experiences, you'll gain a deeper understanding of the strategies that work best for you, without the risk of costly trial and error.

Join me on this journey, and let our characters navigate the complexities of real estate investing alongside you. Together, we'll explore the most effective strategies, avoid common pitfalls, and unlock the secrets to success in the world of real estate.

All Bets Are On: Welcome to the Real Estate Game, Where Everyone Wins!

As we embark on this journey together, I want to assure you that there's room for every kind of investor. Whether you're a seasoned pro or just starting out, whether you're hands-on or hands-off, this book has valuable insights tailored just for you.

Your unique character profile—whether it's Noah, Alex, Peyton, Sam, or Logan—has a place in the world of real estate. Your adventure awaits, and it's time to take the first step.

So, let's get started!

Chapter 1

The ROI Riddle—How to Calculate It and How to Improve It

Measuring the success of a real estate investment is crucial for investors, developers, and property owners. Probably the most important metric used to evaluate the profitability of a real estate venture is return on investment (ROI). ROI is a widely accepted benchmark that helps investors determine whether their investment is generating sufficient returns relative to its cost.

In this chapter, we will dive into the concept of ROI in real estate, exploring its definition, calculation methods, and application in various investment scenarios. We will also discuss the factors that influence ROI, such as property type, location, and market conditions. By understanding ROI, real estate investors and professionals can make informed decisions, optimize their investment strategies, and maximize their returns.

While the basic concept of ROI remains the same across asset classes, its application and characteristics differ significantly between real estate and stocks or other investments. Here are some key similarities and differences.

Similarities
- **Basic ROI calculation:** The fundamental ROI formula (gain from investment ÷ cost of investment) applies to all asset classes, including real estate, stocks, and bonds.
- **Performance measurement:** ROI serves as a benchmark to evaluate the performance of an investment, regardless of the asset class.

Differences

- **Cash flow considerations:** Real estate investments often generate rental income or cash flow, which can impact ROI calculations. Stocks and bonds typically provide dividend or interest income, but it's not always a direct cash flow.
- **Appreciation vs. income:** Real estate investments can appreciate in value over time, providing a potential long-term return. Stocks and bonds may also appreciate, but their primary return often comes from income (dividends or interest).
- **Illiquidity:** Real estate investments are generally less liquid than stocks or bonds, making it more difficult to quickly sell or exit the investment.
- **Leverage and financing:** Real estate investments often involve leverage (mortgages or loans), which can amplify returns but also increase risk. Stocks and bonds typically don't involve leverage in the same way.
- **Tax implications:** Real estate investments are subject to unique tax implications, such as depreciation and property taxes, which can impact ROI calculations. Stocks and bonds have different tax implications, such as capital gains taxes.
- **Risk and volatility:** Real estate investments can be less volatile than stocks, but they come with unique risks, such as market fluctuations, tenant vacancies, and property management challenges.

Overall, while the basic idea of ROI is the same across investments, real estate has its own set of characteristics that set it apart.

Portfolio Pulse Check: Monitoring Your Investments' Heartbeat

To calculate ROI, you can use two primary methods: the cost method and the out-of-pocket method. The cost method calculates ROI by dividing the investment gain by the total costs related to the property, including purchase price and any repairs to the property.

The out-of-pocket method, on the other hand, calculates ROI based on the equity invested in a property, which can showcase a higher ROI due to leverage.

Cost Method

ROI = investment gain ÷ total costs

Where:
Investment gain = sales price - total costs
Total costs = purchase price + repairs + other costs

ROI = (sales price - purchase price - repairs - other costs) ÷ (purchase price + repairs + other costs)

Out-of-Pocket Method

ROI = investment gain ÷ equity invested

Where:
Investment gain = sales price - outstanding mortgage balance - selling costs
Equity invested = down payment + repairs + other out-of-pocket expenses

ROI = (sales price - outstanding mortgage balance - selling costs) ÷ (down payment + repairs + other out-of-pocket expenses)

For instance, let's say you buy a rental property for $750,000 in cash, and it generates $60,000 in yearly rental income, with $26,000 in annual costs. Using the cost method, your ROI would be 4.5 percent. However, if you finance the property with a loan and invest only $100,000 as a down payment, your ROI using the out-of-pocket method would be 34 percent.

Scenario 1: Cash Purchase (Cost Method)

Investment gain = yearly rental income - annual costs
= $60,000 - $26,000
= $34,000

ROI = investment gain ÷ total costs
= \$34,000 ÷ \$750,000
= 0.045 or 4.5%

Scenario 2: Financed Purchase (Out-of-Pocket Method)

Assume the same income and costs, and ignore loan interest and other financing costs for simplicity.

Investment gain = yearly rental income - annual costs
= \$60,000 - \$26,000
= \$34,000

ROI = investment gain ÷ equity invested (down payment)
= \$34,000 ÷ \$100,000
= 0.34 or 34%

When evaluating ROI, it's essential to consider factors like property type, interest rates, inflation rates, property risk profile, and investor preference. A good benchmark is to compare a potential real estate investment's return with other investments, such as the average stock market return or real estate investment trusts (REITs).

A real estate investment trust (REIT) lets you invest in properties without managing them. REITs are a good benchmark because they're liquid, transparent, and provide steady income, making it easy to compare performance with other investments.

A good ROI in real estate varies depending on factors like location, property type, investment strategy, and market conditions. But there are some general guidelines that can help you determine a figure for your investment.

- **Rental properties:** 8–12 percent annual ROI is considered good, but 15–20 percent or higher can be achieved in high-demand areas or with value-added strategies
- **Fix-and-flip projects:** 15–25 percent ROI or higher is common, but this strategy comes with higher risks and requires significant expertise

- **Wholesale deals:** 10–20 percent ROI or higher can be achieved, but this strategy involves finding undervalued properties and quickly assigning contracts
- **REITs:** 4–8 percent annual ROI is typical, but some REITs can offer higher returns, especially those focused on specific sectors like technology or health care

Keep in mind that these are general benchmarks, and a good ROI ultimately depends on your individual investment goals, risk tolerance, and market conditions.

Logic vs. Love: The Two Faces of Real Estate Returns

To objectively evaluate real estate investments, we'll examine return through a logical lens. Outside of the cost method and the out-of-pocket method ROI calculations, there are four fundamental formulas used to help supplement your ROI calculations for real estate investments. Each of the formulas listed below will build off each other. These four formulas give us a clear picture on the profitability of the deal.

You purchase a rental property in a stable suburb for $750,000. The property generates an annual rental income of $60,000.

1. Gross yield: A simple calculation of annual rental income divided by the property's purchase price.

To calculate the gross yield, I use the following formula:
Gross yield = annual rental income ÷ purchase price
Gross yield = $60,000 ÷ $750,000
Gross yield = 8%

In this example, the gross yield is 8 percent, indicating that you can expect to generate 8 percent of the property's purchase price in annual rental income.

This calculation provides a simple and quick snapshot of the property's potential return, helping you evaluate whether this investment aligns with your goals and expectations.

2. Net operating income (NOI): A more detailed calculation of annual rental income minus operating expenses, divided by the property's purchase price.

For this formula, you will need to take the operating expenses into consideration. For the sake of this example, let's say your operating expenses include:

- Property taxes: 1% of $750,000 = $7,500
- Insurance: $3,500
- Maintenance: $6,000
- Property management: 8% of $60,000 = $4,800
- Utilities: $4,000

Total annual operating expenses:
$7,500 + $3,500 + $6,000 + $4,800 + $4,000 = $26,000 (rounded up from $25,800)

To calculate the NOI, subtract the total annual operating expenses from the annual rental income.
NOI = annual rental income - total annual operating expenses
NOI = $60,000 - $26,000
NOI = $34,000

With an NOI of $34,000, you can see that the investment has the potential to generate a return of $34,000 per year.

3. Capitalization rate (cap rate): A measure of a property's annual NOI divided by its purchase price, expressed as a percentage.

Let's calculate cap rate for the above example.
Cap rate = NOI ÷ purchase price
Cap rate = $34,000 ÷ $750,000
Cap rate = 4.53%

In this example, the cap rate is 4.53 percent. This means that you can expect to generate a 4.53 percent return on your investment each year, based on the property's NOI.

To put this into perspective, if you had invested $750,000 in a different asset, such as a bond or a stock, you would want to earn a similar or higher return to justify the investment. The cap rate provides a useful benchmark for comparing the potential ROI across different assets.

It's also worth noting that cap rates can vary depending on factors such as:

- Location: Properties in high-demand areas tend to have lower cap rates
- Property type: Different types of properties, such as apartments or office buildings, can have different cap rates
- Market conditions: Cap rates can fluctuate based on changes in interest rates, economic conditions, and other market factors

4. Cash-on-cash return (CoC): A calculation of annual cash flow divided by the total cash invested in the property, expressed as a percentage.

Let's say you purchased the property with a 25 percent down payment ($187,500).

As a reminder, your rental income is $60,000 and the operating expenses are:

- Property taxes: 1% of $750,000 = $7,500
- Insurance: $3,500
- Maintenance: $6,000
- Property management: 8% of $60,000 = $4,800
- Utilities: $4,000
- Total annual operating expenses: $26,000

Here's the calculation:
Annual cash flow = total annual rental income - total annual operating expenses - annual mortgage payments

Assuming an annual mortgage payment of $27,402 (based on a 25-year amortization and 4 percent interest rate), the annual cash flow would be:
Annual cash flow = $60,000 - $26,000 - $27,402 = $6,598

To calculate the cash-on-cash return, I'll use the following formula:
Cash-on-cash return = annual cash flow ÷ total cash invested

Total cash invested = down payment + closing costs (assuming 2% of purchase price)
Total cash invested = $187,500 + $15,000
Total cash invested = $202,500

Cash-on-cash return = $6,598 ÷ $202,500 = 3.25%

In this example, the cash-on-cash return is 3.25 percent, indicating a positive cash flow. This means that you would be generating enough rental income to cover your expenses and earn a return on your investment. As an investor, a cash-on-cash return of 3.29 percent is a relatively attractive return, especially considering the potential for long-term appreciation in property value.

Based on the calculations provided:

1. Gross yield: 8% ($60,000 ÷ $750,000)
2. NOI: $34,000 ($60,000 - $26,000)
3. Cap rate: 4.53% ($34,000 ÷ $750,000)
4. Cash-on-cash return: 3.25% ($6,598 ÷ $202,500)

These four formulas provide a logical framework for evaluating real estate investments and comparing their potential returns. While no single metric tells the full story, combining these calculations allows you to make data-driven choices that align with your financial goals and investment strategy.

When evaluating real estate investments, though, it's essential to consider not only the objective returns but also the subjective returns that an investment can bring. This perspective recognizes that investments can provide benefits beyond just monetary gains. Here are some additional ways to evaluate returns with your portfolio.

- **Personal fulfillment:** Does the investment align with your long-term goal of building a real estate portfolio and generating passive income? Does it fit your growth strategy and personal investment while scaling smartly? Does it meet your *why*?

- **Tax benefits:** Are there tax deductions or credits available that can help reduce your taxable income?
- **Legacy and inheritance:** Can the investment property be passed down to future generations?
- **Diversification and risk reduction:** Does the investment provide a hedge against inflation, market volatility, or other economic risks? (Note that this is for those advanced investors who already have a portfolio containing several properties. If you're New-to-the-Game Noah, you'll be considering diversification across your other investments, such as your 401(k), health savings account, IRA(s), etc.).
- **Lifestyle benefits:** Does the investment property provide a sense of community, convenience, or amenities that enhance your tenants' lifestyle?

For example, let's say the investment property evaluated previously is a triplex. Here is an evaluation of the nonmonetary benefits this property provides.

- **Personal fulfillment:** This supports my goal as a longtime real estate investor by adding a new property to my portfolio that I can self-manage and provide an incredible experience to my tenants
- **Tax benefits:** I can deduct the mortgage interest, property taxes, and operating expenses from my taxable income
- **Legacy and inheritance:** The triplex can be passed down to future generations, providing a lasting legacy
- **Diversification and risk reduction:** The investment provides a hedge against inflation and market volatility, as real estate values and rental income tend to increase over time
- **Lifestyle benefits:** The triplex provides a sense of community and convenience, with three separate units that can be rented to tenants

By considering these qualitative value factors, you can make a more well-rounded evaluation of whether a property has a strong potential for returns, not just financially but also personally.

Uncovering Real Estate's Hidden Value

When evaluating returns on investment, it's easy to focus solely on financial gains. However, I firmly believe that the intangible benefits of real estate investing are just as valuable, if not more so.

Consider the following:

- The professional network you build through collaborations and partnerships
- The sense of community and camaraderie that comes with working alongside like-minded individuals
- The meaningful relationships you forge with mentors, peers, and mentees
- The personal satisfaction and pride that come from seeing a project through to completion
- The freedom, flexibility, and peace of mind that accompany financial stability

These intangible returns may not be quantifiable in monetary terms, but their value is undeniable. They form the foundation upon which successful businesses and portfolios are built.

As you reflect on your own journey, I encourage you to consider the ways in which these intangible aspects have enriched your life, enhanced your business acumen, and elevated your portfolio's potential. I'd wager that these unseen returns have had a more profound impact than your financial gains alone.

Moving forward, I urge you to keep both the financial and emotional definitions of "return" top of mind. Both are essential, and both hold significant value. By acknowledging and embracing this dual perspective, you'll be better equipped to cultivate a richer, more rewarding investing experience.

Now that we've laid a framework for determining the ROI for your property (while looking at both the qualitative and quantitative factors), let's see how each persona would determine their ROI. You might relate most to Noah right now, but don't skip over Logan's or Peyton's strategies—they might be exactly what you need down the road.

Noah is a beginner investor focused on generating steady cash flow rather than chasing property appreciation. If you're just starting out, following Noah's approach means:

- Targeting markets known for strong rental income.
- Prioritizing properties that pay you month-to-month.
- Using ROI calculations to avoid risky investments.
- Building good financial habits early on.
- Making smart, informed decisions that set you up for long-term success.

Mastering ROI is your first step to understanding your investments and confidently growing your real estate portfolio.

How to Start: Researching Properties and Calculating ROI

1. **Pick a target area**
   Begin by selecting a neighborhood or city where you want to invest. Look for places with strong rental demand, job growth, or other positive indicators.

2. **Research average rents**
   Use online rental platforms, local listings, or property management companies to find out what similar properties rent for in that area. This gives you a baseline for expected income.

3. **Calculate ROI**
   ROI helps you understand how much profit you're making compared to your initial investment. Here are two simple methods to calculate it:

   ○ **Cost method:**
     ROI = annual rental income - annual expenses ÷ total property cost × 100
     Example: If a property costs $300,000, rents for $2,000/month ($24,000/year), and annual expenses (taxes, maintenance, mortgage interest) total $10,000, then:
     ROI = 24,000 - 10,000 ÷ 300,000 × 100 = 4.67%
     ROI = 4.67%

   ○ **Out-of-pocket method:**
     ROI= annual cash flow ÷ cash invested x 100

Example: If you put $50,000 down cash and your monthly cash flow (income minus all expenses including mortgage) is $500 ($6,000/year), then:
ROI = 6,000 ÷ 50,000 × 100 = 12%
ROI = 12%

ACTIVE ALEX

If you're a hands-on investor like Alex, who enjoys being actively involved in renovations, then you'll want to focus on the CoC metric. As an "Active Alex," you're investing not only your money but also your sweat equity into projects. CoC will help you determine how effectively each dollar is working for you, revealing whether you're truly generating cash flow. This metric is particularly crucial when leveraging financing and personal effort to maximize investments, allowing you to optimize your strategy and make informed decisions.

PIVOT PEYTON

If you're like Peyton, who may not have immediate access to personal funds for investing, don't worry! You can explore alternative funding routes, such as syndicating funds from your network, securing bank loans, and partnering with family and friends who are investors. As a flexible and creative investor like Peyton, you'll thrive in situations where market shifts and innovative strategies come into play. In such cases, the cap rate becomes a vital metric for evaluating potential returns. Cap rate helps you assess a property's inherent profitability before factoring in financing, enabling you to pinpoint opportunities where value can be added through creative approaches like subdividing, accessory dwelling units (ADUs), or other optimizations.

SEASONED-INVESTOR SAM

As a seasoned investor like Sam, who prioritizes long-term gains and cash flow, you're likely driven by a desire to build lasting wealth and legacy. With a high-income earning job, you're not reliant on immediate cash flow, allowing you to focus on strategic investments that will yield long-term benefits. To optimize your investment approach, consider dual tracking two key metrics: ROI and cap rate. By evaluating properties from multiple angles and prioritizing strategies that generate long-term wealth, you'll be well positioned to build a lasting legacy and achieve your financial goals.

🕐 LONG-GAME LOGAN

As a forward-thinking investor like Logan, you're considering the long-term financial and personal benefits of real estate. To achieve sustainable success, prioritize calculations that evaluate not only financial returns but also intangible benefits like networking, freedom, and legacy-building. While CoC helps optimize short-term cash flow, don't overlook the value of strategic investments that create stability and lasting wealth. By balancing financial analysis with relationship-driven decision-making, you'll be well on your way to building a thriving real estate portfolio that supports your long-term goals and aspirations.

Chapter 2

Evaluating Performance

No investment is perfect, but with the right strategies, you can unlock hidden potential in your properties and maximize returns. To do that, you'll need to know how to evaluate property performance, implement optimization strategies, and protect your investments for long-term growth and profitability. As a real estate investor, it's essential to be adaptable and open to new ideas. Often, investors get stuck in a familiar pattern, relying on a single strategy that may not be the best fit for every property.

An investor might only focus on long-term rentals with a buy-and-hold strategy, or they might only invest in turnkey properties fit for short-term rentals (STRs). You might be evaluating a property based only on its potential as a fix-and-flip. But there are lots of strategies to choose from that could benefit your portfolio.

It's crucial to think creatively and consider various options for each property in your portfolio. Ask yourself:

- Could this property be better suited for a rental income strategy?
- Might a renovate-and-hold approach yield higher returns?
- Could a wholesale or partnership opportunity be more profitable?

Every property holds potential for untapped equity that can be leveraged to improve performance. By optimizing or changing a property's use, you can unlock hidden value, leading to increased cash flow and appreciation.

For example, three years ago, I converted a triplex from a long-term rental to an Airbnb. Prior to the conversion, the property generated $8,500 in monthly net revenue as a long-term rental. However, after hiring an Airbnb property manager and investing in necessary upgrades (such as furniture), the property's monthly net revenue soared to $11,000, resulting in an impressive annual increase of $27,000.

I've found that there are four clear steps to evaluating property performance.

1. **Analyze return metrics:** Examine CoC, cap rate, and overall ROI to assess a property's performance. For example, you can analyze your return metrics on your current portfolio once a year after tax season, since you'll have all of your paperwork and hard numbers in front of you. An annual review will help you make sure your portfolio is healthy—and strategize how to make it perform even better or take it from red to green if a property is underperforming.

2. **Consider risk exposure:** Risk in real estate investing refers to potential financial losses or reduced returns due to market fluctuations, vacancies, unexpected expenses, mortgage risks, or tenant issues. To mitigate these risks, investors can focus on reducing expenses, increasing income, and paying off mortgages quickly, helping to protect their investments and achieve more stable returns.

3. **Track performance over time:** Monitor property performance and adjust your strategies accordingly. You'll want to look for things like reducing vacancies and increasing tenancy, what expenses you can reduce (like adjusting property management fees, landscaping and yard maintenance, switching to a different energy provider, updating appliances to be more energy efficient to reduce costs, etc.), while minimizing expenses.

4. **Optimize opportunity cost:** Opportunity cost here refers to potential losses from vacancy, such as lost rental income and increased marketing costs. By proactively communicating with tenants, landlords can minimize vacancy periods and reduce these losses, maximizing their returns.

When you follow this process, you can make informed decisions about your property and unlock its full potential. Just like in the triplex example, small changes—whether adjusting your rental strategy, optimizing expenses, or exploring new revenue streams—can lead to significant financial gains. The key is to stay proactive.

Portfolio Powerplay: Optimizing for Maximum Impact

Once you've determined the performance of your property with these steps, you'll transition into safeguarding your investments. You'll want to safeguard against market volatility and unexpected events, making them bulletproof and profitable in unstable conditions. To achieve this, I've focused on two key strategies that have proven effective in my own portfolio: optimizing and scaling.

Optimizing existing properties can help you protect your investments, especially during economic downturns, when interest rates rise, or when the market slows. Here are three effective strategies that have worked for me.

- **Renovate to increase income potential.** Renovating a property can significantly boost its income potential. By upgrading amenities and appliances, enhancing curb appeal, adding extra bedrooms or bathrooms, creating an open floor plan, and installing smart home features, you can increase rental income, attract higher-paying tenants, and boost property value. Strategic renovations can make a property more desirable, leading to increased revenue and a stronger bottom line.
- **Convert properties to STRs.** Converting properties to STRs can be a lucrative strategy, especially in high-demand areas. By listing properties on platforms like Airbnb, VRBO, or HomeAway; targeting specific demographics; offering additional services; and optimizing pricing and occupancy rates, you can increase revenue, reduce vacancy rates, and diversify your income streams. STRs can provide a higher ROI compared to traditional long-term rentals, making it an attractive option for investors.
- **Explore value-add opportunities.** Exploring value-add opportunities can help unlock hidden value in your properties. This can include adding ADUs, building out basements or attics, creating outdoor living spaces, installing solar panels or energy-efficient systems, and pursuing zoning changes or variances. By identifying

and capitalizing on these opportunities, you can increase property value, attract higher-paying tenants, and boost cash flow, ultimately strengthening your investment portfolio.

If your portfolio is optimized, you might consider scaling. However, do it cautiously and only when it fits your strategy and risk tolerance. Scaling requires experience, resources, and capital, so grow at a pace that works for you. Here are three effective strategies to consider when scaling your portfolio.

- Utilizing a 1031 exchange is a highly effective strategy for deferring capital gains taxes on investment properties. (We'll go into much more detail on this in Chapter 12.) By swapping one property for another, investors can reinvest their profits without incurring taxes on the gain. This powerful tool offers numerous benefits, including the ability to defer capital gains taxes, reinvest proceeds in a new property, diversify your portfolio, and increase cash flow and returns. For instance, if an investor sells a property for $1 million and uses a 1031 exchange to purchase a new property worth $1.2 million, they can defer paying taxes on the $200,000 gain. This can result in thousands of dollars in tax savings, allowing the investor to reinvest their profits in a new property, ultimately fueling further growth and success.
- Similarly, an investor could trade an underperforming or stagnant property for one with better returns. For example, if an investor owns a property generating $10,000 per month in rental income but identifies a new property with the potential to generate $15,000 per month, swapping properties can yield an impressive $5,000 monthly increase in cash flow.
- Renovating or adding units to existing properties is a highly effective way to unlock hidden value and significantly increase income potential. By upgrading or expanding existing properties, investors can enhance their appeal, boost property value, and attract higher-paying tenants. For instance, renovating a two-bedroom,

one-bathroom property by adding an extra bedroom and bathroom can substantially increase its value and appeal, allowing investors to command higher rents and boost their returns.

As you begin to evaluate your portfolio, you'll be able to identify areas to optimize your real estate investments. By thinking outside of the box and exploring these innovative ways to maximize your property's ROI, you'll be able to create profit in any market. Beyond traditional rental strategies, you'll be able to consider converting a home into a lucrative STR, renting individual rooms for added income, or tapping into niche markets like adult family homes (AFHs), which provide specialized care for small groups of seniors. These unconventional approaches can significantly boost your property's earning potential, and being aware of all your options will help you make smart decisions as you potentially pivot your strategy. Stay tuned for in-depth discussions on each of these exciting opportunities in upcoming chapters.

Case Study: From Humble Home to High-Yielding Haven

I bought a distressed single-family house in Shoreline, a suburb of Seattle. The house had a unique layout, featuring two stories and a second kitchen in the basement. At first, I just renovated the property because my initial strategy was to just fix-and-flip (more on this strategy in Chapter 10), but when it was time to list, I realized that this house had massive potential. I ended up dividing the house into two units, converting the garage into a third unit, and increasing the footprint of the house from 3,200 square feet to 4,400 square feet. I also took it from a four-bedroom house to a ten-bedroom house. This renovation opened up new possibilities for generating income.

Before:

After:

Ultimately, I opted to convert the property into a lucrative Airbnb, earning $20,000 per month in gross income—a significant increase from the $8,000 I would have earned through traditional renting.

Here's a breakdown of the numbers:

- Purchase price: $585,000
- Renovation costs: $175,000
- Addition: $180,000
- Airbnb setup: $100,000

After refinancing the property, it now generates $5,000 in monthly cash flow as an Airbnb after all expenses paid. The most impressive outcome, however, is the property's appreciation in value. It went from $585,000 to $1.8 million in just three years—while maintaining steady cash flow!

Essential Questions to Maximize Your Portfolio's Value

To optimize your real estate investments, it's essential to think beyond traditional approaches and identify hidden opportunities within your portfolio. Whether you're looking to boost cash flow, increase property value, or explore alternative uses, asking the right strategic questions can lead you in the right direction. Consider the following questions as a road map to uncover new possibilities and elevate your real estate strategy.

- **Expansion opportunities:** Can you add more square footage to the property to increase its value and rental income?
- **Alternative uses:** Are there alternative uses for the property, such as:
  - STRs (e.g., Airbnb).
  - Rent-by-room models.
  - AFH.
  - Other niche markets (student housing, artist or maker spaces, etc.).
- **Subdivision potential:** Can the lot be subdivided to create additional properties, increasing overall value and potential income?
- **Zoning opportunities:** Can the zoning be changed to allow for:

- Commercial use.
- Higher density development.
- Other uses that could increase property value and income.

- **Renovation and upgrade potential:** Can renovations or upgrades increase the property's value, such as:
  - Modernizing outdated features.
  - Adding energy-efficient systems.
  - Enhancing curb appeal.

- **Cash flow optimization:** Are there opportunities to optimize cash flow, such as:
  - Increasing rental rates.
  - Reducing operating expenses.
  - Implementing cost-saving technologies.

- **Tax efficiency:** Are there tax-efficient strategies to explore, such as:
  - Depreciation and amortization.
  - Tax-deferred exchanges (1031 exchanges).
  - Other tax-advantaged approaches.

- **Financing options:** Are there alternative financing options available, such as:
  - Refinancing existing loans.
  - Exploring new loan products (e.g., interest-only loans).
  - Partnering with investors or private lenders.

- **Market trends and demand:** What are the current market trends and demand drivers in the area, and how can you capitalize on them?

- **Long-term strategy:** What is your long-term strategy for the property, and how does it align with your overall investment goals and risk tolerance?

Unlocking the Full Potential of Your Real Estate Portfolio

As we conclude this chapter, it's clear that maximizing the potential of your real estate portfolio requires a strategic and multifaceted approach. By asking the right questions and exploring alternative uses, expansion opportunities, and tax-efficient strategies, you can unlock hidden value and increase your returns.

Remember, every property is unique, and what works for one investment may not work for another. It's essential to stay adaptable, monitor market trends, and continually assess your portfolio's performance.

By applying the insights and strategies outlined in this chapter, you'll be better equipped to:

- Identify opportunities to increase cash flow and property value.
- Optimize your portfolio's performance and minimize risk.
- Stay ahead of the curve in a rapidly changing real estate market.

Let's take a moment to revisit our *Choose Your Own Adventure* characters and their suggested actions. Review each scenario and consider the next steps for your own real estate journey.

NEW-TO-THE-GAME NOAH

Now that you've learned the fundamentals of real estate investing, it's time to apply them to your first property. Using the metrics explained in Chapter 1, evaluate your property's:

- Cash-on-cash return
- Cap rate
- ROI

This exercise will help you:

- Reinforce your understanding of key concepts.
- Develop a data-driven approach to investing.
- Make informed decisions about your property.

To ensure you're on the right track, consider seeking guidance from a mentor or experienced investor. Ask them to review your calculations and provide feedback on your concluded actions.

Their expertise can help you:

- Avoid costly mistakes.
- Maximize your property's potential.
- Refine your investment strategy.

Don't be afraid to ask for help. Guidance from experienced investors can be a game changer in your real estate journey. I still run some of my deals, design choices, comps, etc. with other investors in my network.

🔨 ACTIVE ALEX

Now that you've evaluated your property's key metrics, it's time to explore opportunities to boost its performance. Consider hands-on projects that can increase rental income, such as:

- Adding a unit or converting underutilized spaces.
- Upgrading appliances, fixtures, and finishes to attract higher-paying tenants.
- Enhancing curb appeal and exterior amenities.

Beyond physical renovations, think about changing the property's use to increase cash flow. Ask yourself:

- Could converting a rental into a short-term vacation property (e.g., Airbnb) generate higher returns?
- Are there opportunities to repurpose underutilized spaces, such as a garage or attic, into additional rental units?
- Could a change in property use, such as converting a residential property into a commercial or mixed-use space, unlock new revenue streams?

By identifying and executing strategic renovations and upgrades, you can:

- Increase rental income and cash flow.
- Enhance property value and appreciation.
- Stay competitive in a rapidly changing real estate market.

💡 PIVOT PEYTON

It's time to get creative and explore nontraditional strategies to take your portfolio to the next level. Consider the following innovative approaches:

- **Subdividing a lot:** Can you split a large lot into smaller parcels, creating opportunities for additional development or sales?
- **Adding an ADU:** Can you build an ADU, such as a backyard cottage or garage conversion, to increase rental income?
- **Niche rentals:** Can you convert a home into a specialized rental, such as:
  - Senior living.
  - STRs (e.g., Airbnb).
  - Student housing.
  - Artist or maker spaces.

Assess your current market conditions and ask yourself:

- Is the market shifting, and is it time to pivot?
- Are there emerging trends or opportunities that you can capitalize on?
- Can you adjust your strategy to improve your property's performance and maximize returns?

Don't be afraid to think outside the box and explore unconventional strategies. By doing so, you can:

- Stay ahead of the competition.
- Increase cash flow and returns.
- Build a unique and resilient portfolio that's poised for long-term success.

SEASONED-INVESTOR SAM

As a savvy investor, it's time to tap into the hidden potential of your properties. Focus on leveraging untapped equity to propel your investments to new heights.

Consider refinancing your properties to access the equity you've built up. Use this newfound capital to:

- Acquire additional properties, expanding your portfolio and increasing cash flow.

- Pursue larger, more lucrative deals, amplifying your returns.
- Invest in renovations or upgrades, boosting property values and rental income.

Don't underestimate the power of your professional network. Leverage your connections to:

- Gather fresh insights and ideas on optimizing your portfolio.
- Stay informed about market trends and emerging opportunities.
- Collaborate with fellow investors, sharing knowledge and best practices.

By unlocking the equity in your properties and leveraging your network, you'll be able to:

- Accelerate your investment growth.
- Increase cash flow and returns.
- Stay ahead of the competition in a rapidly changing market.

LONG-GAME LOGAN

To optimize your property portfolio's performance, consider hiring a land-use coach to evaluate your properties for untapped potential. Their expert analysis will help you:

- Identify hidden opportunities for growth.
- Explore alternative uses for your properties.
- Unlock potential for increased cash flow and appreciation.

When reviewing the land-use coach's findings, consider multiple elevated opportunities for each property, such as:

- Subdividing or rezoning to increase property value.
- Repurposing or redeveloping properties to attract higher-paying tenants.
- Implementing sustainable features to enhance property appeal and reduce operating costs.

To maintain a strategic focus, delegate daily management tasks to capable professionals, such as:

- Property managers to oversee daily operations.
- Accounting professionals to handle financial reporting and tax planning.
- Maintenance personnel to ensure properties remain in top condition.

As you delegate tasks, encourage your team to keep a keen eye on:

- Property appreciation and long-term growth.
- Generating stable, long-term returns.
- Sustainability and environmental responsibility.

By leveraging expert advice, delegating tasks, and maintaining a strategic focus, you'll be able to:

- Optimize your property portfolio's performance.
- Achieve sustainable growth and long-term returns.
- Enjoy peace of mind knowing your investments are in capable hands.

Conclusion to Part 1

When you join the realm of real estate, you are given the opportunity to combine your ambition with creativity and grit to find your way to success. Regardless of how challenging the market may feel, there is opportunity out there. Stop doomscrolling Zillow. Quit telling yourself there aren't deals out there. Reframe your perspective and think differently.

It's important to get out there and do it.

After immersing myself in books, podcasts, and strategies, I finally felt equipped to take on the real estate investing world. I mastered key metrics, learned to spot lucrative deals on Zillow, and gained confidence in my abilities. But knowledge alone wasn't enough—I needed to take the plunge! With a surge of determination and a dash of courage, I combined my expertise with ambition and started making moves. The thrill of turning theory into reality was exhilarating! Now, I'm excited to share my journey with you, and one key takeaway stands out: Taking action was the game changer. Regardless of the situation, I pushed forward, and that's what made all the difference.

I still remember the rush of adrenaline as I closed on my first property, a supposed "cosmetic flip" that would launch my real estate investing career. But, as I soon discovered, nothing could have prepared me for the chaos that ensued.

I had bought the house "sight unseen," a rookie mistake that would haunt me for months to come. The real estate broker had assured me it was a gem, but I later realized that was just a clever sales pitch. As I stepped foot into the property for the first time, my heart sank. The house was a disaster.

Every possible issue reared its ugly head: plumbing and electrical problems, mold and dry rot, a leaky basement . . . it was like the property was cursed. My initial optimism quickly turned to despair as I stared at the ever-growing to-do list. This was no cosmetic flip; it was a full-blown renovation nightmare.

Finding a reliable contractor proved to be another challenge. I interviewed fifteen different candidates, each one promising the world but failing to deliver. Time was ticking, and I was getting desperate. Finally, after what felt like an eternity, I found the right person for the job.

But just as we were making progress, another obstacle emerged: We listed the house during the worst possible time, the week of Thanksgiving. The market was dead, and our beautiful renovation was met with crickets. Thirty days passed without a single offer, and I was starting to lose hope.

It wasn't until February of the following year that we finally closed the deal. The numbers were bleak: I had lost around $5,000 on my first venture. It was a hard pill to swallow, but I knew I had survived. I had hustled, optimized, and pushed through the chaos, and that's what mattered.

That first deal was a trial by fire, a baptism into the wild world of real estate investing. But it also taught me the importance of due diligence, perseverance, and creative problem-solving.

I emerged from that experience feeling invincible, like I could conquer anything. Despite the numerous mistakes I made, the lessons I learned were invaluable. They were the kind of insights that can't be gleaned from webinars or podcasts—only from diving in headfirst and getting my hands dirty. One of the most profound takeaways was that nothing—absolutely nothing—replaces the power of hands-on experience.

I want you to pause and think.

- What would you be willing to pay to learn a huge portion of what you needed to know for your new industry or endeavor?
- What would you pay to work with a mentor?
- What would you pay to take an online course?
- What would you pay to go to a week-long conference or retreat?

I can promise you that none of those opportunities compare to actually getting in there and getting the work done. Nothing beats actually being in the situation where you are the decision-maker, where you are the doer. By jumping in with both feet and actually *doing the thing*, I learned a lot of what I needed to know—*fast*.

While losing money is never the goal, I encourage you to reframe it as an investment in your education. This mindset shift can make the initial setbacks more palatable, especially when venturing into your first property—or even your first few.

PART TWO

Change Your Operating Model

As a real estate investor, have you ever stopped to think about the underlying business model driving your investments? Many investors overlook this crucial aspect, treating their rental properties as isolated assets rather than interconnected components of a larger business. However, recognizing and adapting your operating model can be a game changer for your investment strategy.

An operating model defines how you manage and generate revenue from your properties. Just like businesses in other industries, real estate investors can adopt various operating models to suit their goals, risk tolerance, and market conditions. Some common operating models include:

- **Traditional rental model:** Renting properties to tenants through long-term leases.
- **STR model:** Renting properties on platforms like Airbnb, VRBO, or HomeAway.
- **Co-living/rent-by-room model:** Renting individual rooms within a property to multiple tenants. Offering shared living spaces and community-driven amenities.
- **Property management model:** Hiring a third-party property management company to oversee day-to-day operations.

Each operating model presents unique benefits, challenges, and profit potential. By understanding and adapting your operating model, you can unlock new opportunities for growth, improve cash flow, and achieve your investment goals.

Let's explore this concept further. The other day I was at my hair salon, owned by my friend, Joe. While I was getting my hair done, my stylist mentioned that she rented her salon chair from Joe. This made me realize that as the owner, Joe benefited from a few different streams of income offering commission-based services and selling hair products. Similarly, as a real estate investor, you can explore different operating models to maximize your returns and stay competitive in an ever-changing market.

Plus, your goals and priorities are likely to evolve over time. Sticking to a single approach can limit your potential and hinder your progress. Perhaps you're looking to maximize cash flow, navigate changing regulations, or simply achieve a better work-life balance.

By being open to adjusting your operating model, you can:

- Unlock new opportunities for growth and profitability.
- Stay adaptable in an ever-changing market.
- Align your investment strategy with your shifting goals and priorities.

In the following chapters, we'll dive into various operating model changes that can empower you to take control of your investment journey. You'll learn the why, the how, and the best implementation strategies for each model, whether you're acquiring a new property or optimizing your existing portfolio. By the end of this journey, you'll be equipped to choose the model that best suits your needs and aspirations as an investor.

Chapter 3

The Length-of-Stay Showdown

Length of stay as a business model is precisely what it sounds like: changing the average length of time each tenant stays on your property. Will you be renting your property to people on a short-, medium- or long-term basis? Each length involves catering to a different type of tenant or purpose for the property and comes with unique considerations. But the great thing about changing up your length-of-stay strategy is that you often don't have to do much work to the physical property to instate a new model.

Most investors who change their length-of-stay business model will be going from a long-term rental to short- or medium-term rentals, but it might be right for you to make a different change. Let's take an in-depth look at each of the three lengths of stay so you can determine which one will be the most profitable for you and your property.

As we dig into each, it is important to remember that these definitions may vary slightly (depending on your property's local government and laws), so you should always do your due diligence to research the legalities and specifics for each opportunity in your specific market.

Long-Term Rentals

Long-term rentals are considered a "tried and true" strategy and, in general, less effort overall for investors. A long-term rental is a residential property leased for an extended period of time at a fixed monthly rate. Long-term rental units are usually unfurnished and leave the responsibility of utility payments to the tenant rather than the owner or landlord. This length-of-stay model is often preferred by landlords because it provides a stable, consistent income stream, reducing the need for frequent tenant turnover. On the whole, long-term rentals can be more passive, which is appealing. Creating a passive income stream through long-term rentals can be even more hands-off if you hire out the task of property management.

> According to Catherine Reed in an article on housing trends for flex.com, "Approximately 80 percent of people who own and operate rental properties utilize the long-term rental strategy."[1]

But it's not just good for the investor! For tenants, long-term rentals offer the benefits of a more settled living situation, fostering community connections, and allowing for greater personalization of their home. This arrangement often comes with the opportunity to negotiate lease terms, offering tenants more security and peace of mind.

Long-Term Rental Pros

- Stable income streams and predictable cash flow. This allows investors to plan their finances more effectively and make informed decisions about future investments.
- Long-term tenants take better care of properties. They are also more likely to report maintenance issues promptly, reducing the risk of costly repairs.
- There are fewer vacancies and turnovers, which means less work finding and onboarding new tenants.

Long-Term Rental Challenges

- Properties are largely unavailable for owner use. This can be a significant drawback for investors who want to use their properties for personal vacations or other purposes.
- Complex tenant laws and regulations can be challenging to navigate, especially in tenant-friendly states. Investors must carefully research and understand local laws to avoid costly mistakes or disputes with tenants. Squatters, evictions, and nonpaying tenants are becoming quite a nuisance.
- Long-term rentals may be subject to rent-control laws, limiting the amount of rent that can be charged. This can impact cash flow and profitability.

---

[1]   Catherine Reed, "35 Insightful Landlord Statistics – 2023," *Flex* (blog), January 9, 2023, https://getflex.com/blog/landlord-statistics.

While long-term tenants tend to take better care of properties, there is still a risk of damage or neglect—and because tenants turn over less often, you may not find out until months or even years later, when you find yourself facing costly repairs.

Case Study: The Reality of Long-Term Renting

Long-term rentals can be a lucrative investment, but beware; they also come with their own set of headaches, especially in tenant-friendly states like Washington. As a seasoned real estate investor, I thought I'd seen it all. But nothing could have prepared me for the day my property manager delivered the bombshell: A squatter couple was living in my vacant triplex, claiming they had a lease from me—a lease that never existed.

The unit, located in the prestigious Seattle neighborhood of Queene Anne, was worth $3,000 per month in rent—money these strangers weren't paying me. Worse, they were destroying the property. They had ripped out carpets, broken windows, and damaged door jams. I confronted the squatters, but they were defiant, flaunting their fake lease, refusing to leave, and threatening to call their attorney. I knew I had to take drastic measures.

But when I called the Seattle Police Department, they deemed it a civil matter, leaving me to navigate the complex and time-consuming eviction process alone. The squatters took full advantage of the situation, changing their mailing address to receive mail at my property and even decorating for Halloween.

Determined to reclaim my property, I turned to social media, creating a video that exposed the squatters and their antics. The video went viral, garnering over one million views and catching the attention of local media. A news channel reached out to me, and their pressure on the Seattle Police Department helped expedite the eviction process.

With the help of my attorney, we filed a formal request to remove the squatters. Finally, after three weeks of stress and uncertainty, the police arrived, and the squatters were evicted in a dramatic and emotional confrontation.

The aftermath was a whirlwind of insurance claims, renovations, and repairs. But I was determined to turn a negative into a positive. I renovated the entire property, increased rents, and strengthened the value of the building.

Looking back, this experience taught me a harsh lesson about the vulnerability of landlords. But it also showed me the importance of being proactive and taking measures to prevent similar situations in the future. I've since reevaluated my landlord insurance, installed cameras outside vacant units, and increased my property manager's visits to prevent trespassing.

Despite this harrowing experience, I remain committed to investing in long-term rentals in this tenant-friendly state. Why? Because our market's appreciation is unparalleled, and I'm in it for the long haul. I believe that with the right investments, the benefits far outweigh the challenges over time.

Evictions, vacancies, and high insurance costs are undeniable risks, but they can be mitigated with careful planning and management. And let's not forget the silver lining: With each passing month, my long-term tenants are paying down my mortgage, building equity, and increasing my wealth.

Short-Term Rentals

A short-term rental (STR) refers to a legally permitted property, rented for less than thirty days. STRs are typically found in residential or resort areas and come fully furnished. With this length-of-stay model, tenants do not pay for expenses like utilities. Primarily utilized for vacationers, these properties are commonly listed on platforms such as Airbnb, VRBO, Expedia, and a host of other similar online websites.

Unlike hotels and bed-and-breakfasts, STRs can offer a diverse option of accommodations, including private residences, cottages, or cabins, making them appealing to tourists visiting those particular (and often popular!) spots.

The STR market is poised for explosive growth, with projections indicating a valuation of approximately $8.9 billion by 2026.[2] This surge in demand is driven by travelers seeking unique, home-away-from-home experiences and authentic local connections that traditional hotels often can't provide.

The rise of online booking platforms and the increasing popularity of budget-friendly travel options are also fueling this growth. As the STR market continues to expand, savvy investors are taking notice.

---

[2]   David Bitton, "Short-Term Rentals Real Estate Statistics: Will the Market Thrive?" *DoorLoop* (blog), January 9, 2025, https://www.doorloop.com/blog/short-term-rentals-real-estate-statistics#:~:text=this%20booming%20market.-,By%20the%20year%202026%2C%20the%20short%2Dterm%20rental%20market%20is,19.1%25%20from%202022%20to%202032.

Did you know income generated from STRs is classified as active income? For real estate investors, this designation is important because it allows you (the owner) to deduct related expenses and only pay taxes on your profits.

Short-Term Rental Pros

- STRs can generate higher revenue compared to long-term rentals, especially in high-demand areas and during peak travel seasons.
- STRs offer the flexibility to adjust pricing, occupancy, and rental duration in response to changing market conditions.
- With shorter guest stays, there's typically less wear and tear on the property compared to long-term rentals.
- STRs allow owners to use the property themselves when it's not rented, providing a convenient vacation home or weekend getaway.
- STRs may qualify for tax deductions on expenses related to the rental, such as mortgage interest, property taxes, and operating expenses.
- STRs can reduce dependence on a single tenant or rental income source.
- STRs allow owners to set clear boundaries and expectations with guests, minimizing potential conflicts and issues.
- STRs can provide opportunities to offer additional services, such as property management, cleaning, and concierge services, increasing revenue potential.

Short-Term Rental Challenges

- Properties outside popular tourist areas may experience higher vacancies. According to Airbnb's own data, properties in nonpeak areas can have occupancy rates as low as 20–30 percent.
- Short-term guests can cause more damage than long-term tenants. This can result in higher maintenance costs and more frequent renovations.
- Noise and disruptions, which are more common in short-term rentals, can lead to complaints from nearby residents. Implementing quiet hours or noise restrictions can help mitigate these issues.

- Providing essentials like toiletries and cleaning supplies adds to the bottom line. Consider purchasing these items in bulk or using a property management service to help offset costs.
- STRs require frequent cleaning, laundry, and property preparation. Hiring a professional cleaning service can help alleviate some of this burden.
- Guests may not report problems, leading to unnoticed damage. Regular property inspections can help identify and address issues before they become major problems.
- Demand and supply fluctuations in the market can impact profitability. Staying up to date on local market trends and adjusting pricing accordingly can help mitigate these risks.
- Changes in local laws and regulations can affect STRs. Research local regulations and ensure compliance to avoid fines or other penalties.
- It's harder to screen tenants for STRs, and simply verifying guest identities may not ensure their responsible behavior. Consider using additional screening methods, such as guest reviews or references.

According to a report by AllTheRooms, "the nationwide average Airbnb occupancy rate in the United States stands at 48 percent."[3] This means that, on average, Airbnb properties are vacant approximately 52 percent of the time. However, occupancy rates can vary significantly depending on location, property type, and market demand. For instance, data from AirDNA indicates that certain areas, like Oxford, Mississippi and Big Bear, California, have lower occupancy rates, with figures around 34.9 percent and 39.6 percent, respectively."[4] These variations highlight the importance of considering local market conditions when evaluating potential vacancy risks for STR properties.

Unexpected events (think natural disasters, economic downturns, pandemics, or global crises) will often hit STRs the hardest. Developing a contingency plan and diversifying investments can help reduce risk.

To combat seasonal fluctuations, I adapt my STRs by offering medium-term bookings from September to March. This strategic shift

---

[3] "Average Airbnb Occupancy Rates by City [2023]," AllTheRooms, accessed April 22, 2025, https://www.alltherooms.com/resources/articles/average-airbnb-occupancy-rates-by-city/.

[4] Jamie Lane, "Airbnb Occupancy Rate: Highs, Lows, & Calculating Your Own," AirDNA, March 10, 2024, https://www.airdna.co/blog/airbnb-hosting-tips-for-occupancy-in-2023.

helps maintain high occupancy rates during typically slower winter months, ultimately boosting income and ensuring a more consistent revenue stream.

Medium-Term Rentals

If STRs feel too high maintenance and long-term rentals won't bring in cash quickly enough, medium-term rentals will be right up your alley.

Medium-term rentals cover a property that is rented on a month-to-month basis with the option to renew. Stays in a medium-term rental average from thirty days up to a few months or even a year. These rentals are primarily furnished rentals and cater to people looking for temporary housing.

Medium-term rentals are an altered form of long-term renting, so you still need a lease for tenants, but it will be a month-to-month lease.

Medium-term rentals typically command higher rents than long-term leases, as tenants are often willing to pay a premium for the convenience they offer. However, predicting demand for medium-term rentals can be challenging. Unlike long-term rentals or seasonal STRs, medium-term rentals aren't usually as reliable or consistent. This means that while the financial rewards can be significant, there are also risks involved.

A quick note about taxes to keep in mind. If a rental is used thirty days or less, the income is subject to sales and lodging tax. If the rental is more than thirty days, the income is exempt from sales tax and lodging tax. This makes medium-term rentals more attractive for tenants staying for longer periods since these taxes do not apply.

From a tenant's perspective, medium-term rentals can be really good for a lot of different situations and can appeal to a wide variety of people, all who fall into a category of unconventional renters. Let's take a look at all of the possibilities.

- **Students:** Many students attending college do not go to school year-round and therefore do not live in their college town year-round. This means they don't need to rent a space twelve months a year—more like nine—thus making them great candidates for medium-term rentals.

- **Relocation:** People relocating from one geographic location to another often want to opt for the medium-term rental option because they don't have to make a major financial decision without knowing anything about their new town. By renting a place for a few months first, they can get familiar with the city and take their time to understand neighborhoods, city culture, frequent destination locations (school, work, stores, etc.) before they buy a home or commit to a long-term rental.

- **Homeowners in transition:** Let's say a homeowner suffers the unfortunate incident of a fire or damaging water leak. With a medium-term rental, they can have a comfortable place to live while their house is being repaired. They can move back to their own house when the renovations are complete.

- **Temporary work commitments:** The most common renters for this type of rental are people with temporary work commitments who will only be in a location for a brief amount of time. People falling into this category might include traveling nurses, digital nomads, or contractors in town for short-term projects.

- **Snowbirds:** Some people (often retirees) like to rent out a place seasonally in an attempt to escape the extreme heat or cold of the summer and winter weather. Medium-term rentals are a great fit for these individuals—and if you live in a warm area, there will likely be a lot of them!

Just like long- and short-term rentals, medium-term rentals come with their own risks and rewards, compensations and challenges. Because this length-of-stay strategy is in the middle, it's hard to list its qualities as either pros or cons. Perspective on this length-of-stay strategy depends on the range of investment opportunities you are coming from or moving to and will impact the amount of time, money, and effort you'll be spending. For that reason, I'm laying out the particular points to consider without specific "pro" or "con" labels, so you can decide which are which for your personal situation.

Amenities and Guest Supplies

With a medium-term rental, you will need fewer amenities (think soap, coffee, and consumables) than an STR but more than a property you are renting long term. At the very least, you should provide cleaning supplies and at least a week's worth of consumable paper products like toilet paper and paper towels, as well as fully stock the kitchen with dishes, pots and pans, and utensils. Figuring out what to supply can be a little tricky and might require some experimentation. To help you better gauge what you should supply, ask your guests upon arrival and departure: What do you need? What do you wish you had?

Reviews

Reviews are less important for medium-term rentals than STRs, but it's likely that digital nomads and traveling nurses talk to other digital nomads and traveling nurses. Treat your medium-term tenants well, and they just might be your best lead-generation source for future renters.

Maintenance

Medium-term rentals involve more management than long-term rentals but less than short-term rentals. Therefore, you can anticipate a moderate level of maintenance and wear and tear on your property. One way to avoid the maintenance troubles associated with STRs is to do an exit survey with each medium-term renter asking about any property problems. Phrase the questions in a way that promotes your desire to make improvements on the property rather than in a scolding or blaming tone. If people fear they are going to be financially responsible for the problems they mention, they will likely be less forthcoming with helpful information, costing you more in the long run to fix what needs to be fixed.

Tenant Turnover

Medium-term rentals require finding tenants more frequently than long-term rentals, and you usually have to be more active about looking for them than with STRs. You'll also likely see an increase in the amount of time you communicate with tenants simply from the increased number of move-ins and move-outs.

Time Investment

Medium-term rentals require more work than simply listing a property on an Airbnb website, but you don't have as much pressure to cater to the hospitality side of the business. You will have to be more active about finding tenants as well (Furnished Finder is a great tool for finding medium-term rental tenants). Also, if you don't love interior decorating, medium-term rentals might be a great fit for you because the target market for these properties care more about function, location, and convenience than fancy frills.

Income Expectations

Medium-term rentals typically command higher rents than long-term leases, as tenants are often willing to pay a premium for the convenience they offer—namely location. However, predicting demand for medium-term rentals can be challenging. Unlike long-term rentals or seasonal STRs, medium-term rentals have not historically proven to be as reliable or consistent.

Building Relationships

If you are in the business of real estate, relationships are always important, but perhaps most of all with medium-term rentals. Very successful medium-term rental operators build relationships with local insurance companies, hospitals, universities, large employers, and more in an effort to funnel traveling and temporary workers into their properties. It will take time to build up, but once it gets going, it creates a situation where everyone wins: The company has a solid housing recommendation they can happily and easily offer their employees, and the employees have a quick and accessible housing solution to their unique and immediate needs. And you get a steady flow of high-quality tenants. Build a reputation with these institutions as being reliable, fair, and honest and you'll likely have to turn people away!

Insurance

In light of the recent surge in natural disasters, including devastating fires and hurricanes, insurance premiums have skyrocketed. As you weigh your options, it's crucial to factor in the escalating cost of insurance, which should play a significant role in your decision-making process. Insurance requirements for short-term, medium-term, and long-term rentals vary.

For STRs, you'll need STR-specific insurance. This type of insurance provides financial protection against damages, liability, and lost rental income.

Medium-term rentals often require a combination of short-term and long-term rental insurance. You may need to purchase additional coverage or endorsements to your existing policy. Keep in mind that insurance costs vary depending on individual circumstances and location. It's essential to consult with insurance providers to determine the best coverage options and costs for your specific medium-term rental situation.

For long-term rentals you'll need landlord insurance or rental property insurance. This type of insurance covers:

- **Structural damage:** Protection against vandalism, theft, fire, or storms
- **Liability:** Coverage for injuries or damages caused by tenants or their guests
- **Lost rental income:** Protection against loss of rental income due to property damage or other covered events

Keep in mind that insurance requirements may vary depending on your location, property type, and other factors. It's essential to consult with an insurance professional to determine the best coverage for your specific needs.

Tax Considerations

Here's a breakdown of the tax differences between short-term and long-term rentals.

Short-Term Rentals (Less than Thirty Days)
- **Business income:** STR income is considered business income and is subject to self-employment tax.
- **Expenses:** You can deduct business expenses, such as:
  - Mortgage interest.
  - Property taxes.
  - Operating expenses (e.g., utilities, maintenance).
  - Furniture and appliance depreciation.

- **Depreciation:** You can depreciate the property's value over time, but this can be complex and may require a tax professional's guidance.
- **Tax forms:** Report STR income on Schedule C (Form 1040) and pay self-employment tax on Schedule SE (Form 1040).

Long- and Medium-Term Rentals (Thirty Days or More)
- **Passive income:** Long-term rental income is considered passive income and is not subject to self-employment tax.
- **Expenses:** You can deduct expenses, such as:
  - Mortgage interest.
  - Property taxes.
  - Operating expenses (e.g., utilities, maintenance).
- **Depreciation:** You can depreciate the property's value over time, but this can be complex and may require a tax professional's guidance.
- **Tax forms:** Report long-term rental income on Schedule E (Form 1040).

Key Differences
- **Self-employment tax:** STRs are subject to self-employment tax, while long-term rentals are not.
- **Business expense deductions:** STRs allow for more business expense deductions, such as furniture and appliance depreciation.
- **Tax forms:** STRs require Schedule C and Schedule SE, while long-term rentals require Schedule E.

I learned most of this information through my own CPA, so I highly encourage you to consult a tax professional to ensure you're meeting all tax requirements, not to mention taking advantage of available deductions for your specific rental situation.

Which Strategy Will You Choose?

A question I frequently encounter is: Which length of stay offers greater profitability from a business perspective? While profit is a crucial consideration, it's not the only factor to weigh. All three lengths of stay offer unique benefits and drawbacks, catering to different investor objectives, risk tolerance, and lifestyles.

When you think about short-term versus medium- and long-term rentals and which one is better suited for you as the investor, it requires careful consideration of various factors. You'll want to consider the financing goals, the time commitment, and the market dynamics paired with your own risk tolerance.

For example, STRs offer higher cash flow but demand significant involvement and come with higher risks. Long-term rentals provide a stable income stream, reduce vacancy concerns, and require less involvement from the property owner. However, long-term rentals can be subject to legal complexities more often than short- and medium-term rentals (I'm talking about the lease, specifically).

If you're a visual learner, here is a chart that can help you better process this information. Pieces of this information have been spread throughout the chapter, but now that we've had a chance to learn about each length-of-stay model, take a look at all the options side by side. It's a quick and easy way to check out the time and financial investments necessary and also the returns each one can offer.

	Long	Medium	Short
Length of stay	12+ months	1–12 months	Less than 30 days
Property management	10%	20%	25%
Maintenance	Low	Medium	High
Turnover	Low	Medium	High
Insurance	Standard	High	High
Utilities	Tenant pays	Depends on length of stay	Landlord pays
Rental income	Standard	High	High
Parking	Can charge	Can charge	No charge
Pet fee	Can charge	Can charge	Can charge
Vacancy	Low	Medium	High (extremely seasonal)

*Note: The chart above assumes you will be hiring a property manager.

As you embark on this entrepreneurial venture, remember to consider your personal circumstances, including time and energy.

- **Time commitment:** Managing rentals requires hands-on involvement. If you have a demanding nine-to-five job or family responsibilities, time might be your greatest challenge.
- **Energy levels:** Property management can also tax your physical energy reserves. Be honest about your capacity to handle the stresses and demands the situation will require.

Before you enter into a management commitment, reflect on your motivations for entering this space and assess your appetite for adventure. Ask yourself:

- What are my investment goals, and which rental strategy aligns best with them?
- How much risk am I willing to take on, and which approach offers the right balance of risk and reward?
- What kind of lifestyle do I want to maintain, and which rental strategy will allow me to achieve that?

Reassessing Your Portfolio: Is It Time for a Rental Reality Check?

If you already own one or multiple properties, congratulations! Now's the perfect time to reevaluate your investment strategy using the methods outlined above. You might discover that there's a more effective approach than your current one.

There are numerous reasons to reassess and adjust your investment strategy. Perhaps you want to:

- Maximize rental income.
- Reduce management responsibilities.
- Adapt to changing market conditions.
- Explore new investment opportunities.

While reassessing your strategy might seem daunting, it's definitely worth the effort. By exploring alternative length-of-stay models, you can optimize your property's performance and achieve your investment goals.

Let's take a look at how our characters might approach this task.

Making the Shift: Switching Between Short-Term, Medium-Term, and Long-Term Rentals

From Short(er) to Long: Making the Switch

NEW-TO-THE-GAME NOAH

Reason to switch: Noah jumped into STRs hoping for quick returns, but inconsistent bookings and surprise maintenance costs have made it hard to stay ahead. The learning curve has been steeper than expected, and cash flow is tight. Switching to a long-term rental offers Noah a simpler, more stable path to steady income while he builds confidence and learns the basics of property management.

Challenge: Inconsistent returns and high operating costs from short- and medium-term rentals.

Goal: Create stable, predictable income through a long-term rental strategy.

Action items:
- Check local and state laws, zoning, and HOA guidelines to ensure long-term rentals are permitted and compliant
- Use tools like Zillow or Rentometer to analyze rents and recalculate cash flow for lower turnover and more stable income
- Remove short-term extras, add durable furnishings and appliances, and highlight practical features like parking or storage
- Use a solid, state-specific lease (you can find state-specific leases at www.BiggerPockets.com/BookLease), list on long-term rental platforms, and screen tenants for credit, income, and rental history

Reason to switch: Alex thrives on creating beautiful spaces and curating guest experiences—but lately, the hustle of guest turnover and constant upkeep is wearing thin. Despite putting in extra hours, the financial return isn't matching the effort. Long-term rentals allow Alex to still showcase design expertise while securing reliable income with less day-to-day stress.

Challenge: STRs are demanding too much time and energy—between constant turnovers, staging, and guest communication, it's become more work than reward.

Goal: Maintain strong design appeal while creating a more stable, hands-off rental experience with reliable income and lower management demands.

Action items:
- Replace delicate or seasonal decor with timeless, durable, and tenant-friendly materials, focusing on function over theme—think storage, blackout curtains, and neutral palettes
- Remove guest-oriented services and tools, automate rent collection and maintenance, and use a strong lease to clearly outline tenant responsibilities and expectations
- Update listings to appeal to long-term tenants, refresh photos to emphasize comfort and layout, and highlight nearby lifestyle amenities like gyms, coffee shops, or transit
- List on long-term platforms like Zillow and Apartments. com, and offer tenant-friendly options such as pet allowances or flexible furnishing when appropriate

PIVOT PEYTON

Reason to switch: Peyton is all about agility and making data-driven decisions. With travel demand slowing and local competition heating up, STR revenue is dipping. Peyton spots a shift in the market—more people need stable housing. Pivoting to long-term leases in the right units is a smart move to keep returns strong and avoid vacancy losses.

Challenge: STR income has become too inconsistent due to market shifts, regulation changes, or oversaturation. High turnover, rising operational costs, and reduced bookings are hurting returns.

Goal: Maximize cash flow and reduce risk by adapting to local market conditions and shifting to a stable, long-term rental model that offers more predictable income with lower management overhead.

Action items:

- Review STR regulations and local demand trends using tools like AirDNA or Redfin, and recalculate ROI for a twelve-month lease, comparing it directly to your current short-term income
- Remove STR features like guest books and toiletries, simplify or remove furnishings, and upgrade essentials like laundry, full kitchen tools, and durable finishes
- Draft a clear lease with terms on rent, deposits, maintenance, and renewals; use digital tools to streamline screening, lease signing, and rent collection
- List on long-term platforms like Zillow and Apartments. com, tailor your messaging to renters seeking stability, and build referral relationships with local employers and relocation agents

SEASONED-INVESTOR SAM

Reason to switch: Sam has been in the game long enough to know when it's time to recalibrate. Managing STRs across multiple properties is becoming more trouble than it's worth. Long-term rentals help Sam streamline operations, reduce volatility, and free up time to focus on higher-level investment strategy. It's about maximizing performance with less friction.

Challenge: Managing multiple STRs has become operationally intensive and inefficient. Rising regulation, staffing needs, and variable income are slowing down portfolio growth and increasing risk exposure.

Goal: Optimize portfolio performance by creating more consistent, scalable cash flow with long-term rentals—reducing active management and increasing efficiency across assets.

Action items:
- Identify underperforming STRs and reallocate them to long-term leases for more predictable income; centralize operations like rent collection and lease management to reduce overhead
- Analyze each property for its best use—some may stay STRs, while others perform better as long-term rentals; simplify units with durable finishes and reduce downtime with move-in incentives
- Consolidate or replace property managers with long-term specialists to improve consistency, cut costs, and streamline communications across the portfolio
- Leverage tax strategies like depreciation and 1031 exchanges, track NOI, and evaluate success based on cash flow stability, appreciation, and equity growth over time

LONG-GAME LOGAN

Reason to switch: Logan enjoys the steady flow of income from medium-term stays, but shifts in demand and tightening regulations are starting to cause concern. With an eye on the future, Logan sees long-term rentals as a way to protect income, reduce management involvement, and stay compliant with evolving local rules—all while maintaining a passive income lifestyle.

Challenge: Logan's medium- and short-term rental strategy has become harder to sustain due to shifting demand, rising insurance costs, and stricter local regulations. The income has been solid—but increasingly unstable, and less passive than expected.

Goal: Build a hands-off, dependable income stream by converting select properties into long-term rentals—prioritizing lower effort, reduced risk, and consistent returns aligned with a long-term wealth-building strategy.

Action items:

- Remove high-maintenance STR features like guest supplies and frequent cleanings, replace furnishings with durable or unfurnished options, and install low-upkeep fixtures like LED lighting and vinyl floors
- Automate rent collection and maintenance via platforms like Hemlane, draft a strong lease with clear terms, and consider offering eighteen-to-twenty-four-month leases with move-in incentives
- Screen tenants carefully for stability, and add rent-ready upgrades like home office space, in-unit laundry, or pet-friendly policies to attract quality long-term renters
- Shift your financial focus from nightly cash flow to long-term equity growth, refinance where it improves cash flow, and track returns based on appreciation, debt pay down, and overall stability

From Long to Short (or Medium): How to Make a Smooth Transition

NEW-TO-THE-GAME NOAH

Reason to switch: Noah has gained confidence managing a long-term rental and is ready to increase cash flow. After learning the basics, he sees that STRs in his market can double his monthly income.

Challenge: He's unfamiliar with guest turnover, furnishing expectations, and STR regulations.

Goal: Learn the STR model and create a profitable, well-reviewed unit that boosts income.

Action steps:

- Research local laws and STR licensing requirements
- Furnish the unit with essentials, safety features, and guest-friendly design
- Create a strong online listing with quality photos and a compelling description
- Set up cleaning, turnover, and guest communication systems

ACTIVE ALEX

Reason to switch: Alex is craving more creative control and wants to tap into hospitality-inspired design. The flexibility of STRs fits Alex's passion for staging and curating guest experiences.

Challenge: The up-front cost of furnishing and the ongoing effort of guest management can be draining.

Goal: Turn one unit into a highly reviewed, beautifully branded STR to generate higher returns and showcase design talent.

Action steps:
- Design and furnish the space for visual impact and guest comfort
- Hire a cleaning team and use software for automated booking and guest messaging
- Build a strong brand presence on Airbnb and other platforms
- Track occupancy and guest feedback to refine over time

PIVOT PEYTON

Reason to switch: Peyton has identified a shift in the local market—tourism is on the rise, and STRs are in demand. Always quick to adapt, Peyton sees an opportunity to boost ROI.

Challenge: Pivoting takes capital (furnishings, supplies) and time to learn the ins and outs of hospitality.

Goal: Test the STR model on one property to diversify the portfolio and maximize profit during peak seasons.

Action steps:
- Analyze seasonal pricing trends and STR occupancy rates using tools like AirDNA
- Furnish the property based on guest expectations (not personal taste)
- Use dynamic pricing tools to stay competitive
- Leverage guest reviews to build trust and boost visibility

SEASONED-INVESTOR SAM

Reason to switch: Sam owns a prime location property that's been underperforming as a long-term rental. With the right setup, it could significantly outperform as an STR.

Challenge: Managing STRs doesn't scale well across Sam's portfolio, and he doesn't want to dilute focus.

Goal: Pilot an STR with third-party management to explore a new profit stream without increasing workload.

Action steps:
- Hire a top-rated STR property manager
- Renovate selectively to create a high-end, guest-ready space
- Track key metrics: nightly rate, occupancy, and NOI compared to previous lease model
- Use the results to determine whether to replicate elsewhere

LONG-GAME LOGAN

Reason to switch: Logan sees that a personal use property or seasonal rental has potential as a high-performing STR during parts of the year. Passive income is still the goal—but with a twist.

Challenge: Logan wants minimal involvement and needs to avoid burnout from high-touch guest management.

Goal: Create a hybrid model—short-term during peak season, personal use or medium-term in off months.

Action steps:
- Outsource cleaning and guest communication to a cohost or management company
- Create a seasonal calendar and block off owner use dates
- Invest in durable, stylish furnishings that hold up to frequent turnover
- Monitor annualized return vs. long-term lease to ensure it's worth the switch

Conclusion: Finding Your Perfect Rental Match

As we conclude this chapter, remember that all three length-of-stay strategies—short-term, medium-term, and long-term rentals—can be profitable ventures when executed effectively and tailored to your unique situation; it just takes a little time and reflection to pick the one that will work best for you.

- **Assess your priorities:** Evaluate your personal preferences, risk tolerance, and investment goals.
- **Choose the right strategy:** Select the rental approach that best aligns with your circumstances.

By carefully considering these factors, you'll be well on your way to creating a successful rental investment portfolio that meets your needs and achieves your financial goals.

Chapter 4

Room for Profit—Rent-by-Room and Student Housing

Beyond choosing the ideal length of stay for your rentals, another key consideration can significantly impact your investment strategy: the type of rental unit itself. Specifically, renting out individual rooms instead of entire properties can offer unique benefits and opportunities. In this chapter, we'll explore the ins and outs of rent-by-room and student housing, providing insights on how to capitalize on these niche markets.

The rent-by-room strategy is a versatile approach to renting out individual bedrooms within a shared property. This model offers a unique blend of affordability, flexibility, and customization. Tenants enjoy private rooms while sharing common areas, kitchens, and bathrooms.

In this strategy, each tenant signs their own lease, typically for six to twelve months, providing a stable and reliable income stream for landlords. Some operators prefer month-to-month leases, which can still attract long-term tenants. This flexibility allows landlords to adapt to changing market conditions.

The rent-by-room model caters to a diverse demographic seeking affordable housing options. These rooms often represent the most cost-effective way for individuals to rent a space. As a result, there's usually a steady demand for this type of accommodation in most cities. This demand is driven by various demographics, including young professionals, airport and hospital workers, college and graduate students, and restaurant workers and food service professionals.

By understanding the needs and preferences of these demographics, landlords can tailor their rent-by-room offerings to meet the demand for affordable, flexible housing solutions.

Why Rent-by-Room Rocks

The rent-by-room model is a strategy that many investors like because it's a "Goldilocks" solution. It takes less effort to manage than short- and medium-term rentals, yet it still cash flows better than a standard long-term rental. It also usually utilizes a standard single-family home (SFH), so you don't have to buy larger properties to host multiple tenants—and you can easily increase the value when rehabbing the property. Additionally, you have several options for managing the property, with self-management being highly accessible for this strategy.

Typically, you won't need any high-end furnishings or appliances in a rent-by-room house. It just needs to be clean and work well. The layout can even be a bit funky, decreasing your need to tear down walls with a massive renovation. As long as tenants can easily access the living area and there are bathrooms near all the bedrooms, you should be good to go.

Similarly, you don't need to totally furnish the property as you would with short- and medium-term rentals. You could simply furnish the living space with a couch, chair(s), dining area, and TV. Bedrooms can be unfurnished. I know some rent-by-room operators who do furnish bedrooms on occasion, but your tenants might prefer a specific bed or mattress or desk, which could cause issues if you have to store the furnishings you offered.

Another advantage of this strategy is the consistency and reliability of rent. You can achieve higher rental income similar to short- and medium-term rentals but with more certainty, as occupancy isn't as much of an issue. Even if one tenant stops paying, you'll still have rent coming in from the other tenants. Instead of losing 100 percent of your income if a single tenant defaults, you'd only lose around 25 percent. This diversification helps protect your investment by spreading the risk across multiple tenants.

Perhaps the greatest feature of this strategy is that you have multiple exit strategies when it comes time to sell. You can sell it to someone who wants to keep it as a turnkey rent-by-room house, you can market it as is, or you can "flip" it back to a single-family house to match the nicest comps in the neighborhood.

Case Study

Investing in rent-by-room properties offers a unique opportunity to unlock significant potential for growth and returns. To illustrate this, I'd like to share an inspiring example from my friends and fellow investors Christian and Shannon Nossum.

Christian and Shannon have been successfully leveraging the rent-by-room strategy in Seattle for over twenty years. Their journey began when Shannon was still an undergraduate at the University of Washington, and Christian was just twenty-two years old. They took the bold step of purchasing their first student housing property, a duplex in Seattle near the University of Washington. They lived in the two-bedroom upper unit apartment while renting out the seven-bedroom lower unit to college students. Because Christian and Shannon were willing to share their space, they actually made positive cash flow each month living in their own house.

In the following years, they went on to purchase a number of other student housing properties near the University of Washington. These units ranged from two to eleven bedrooms. Some of the units Shannon and Christian bought were already optimized for the rent-by-room strategy, but many of the homes they purchased needed remodeling and renovation to accommodate more bedrooms.

More bedrooms equals more tenants. More tenants equals more rent. More rent equals more cash flow.

The Nossums self-manage all of their properties, run a real estate broker team, have a podcast, do house flips and new builds, and have three awesome children, proving this is absolutely an achievable strategy for investors with a busy lifestyle.

The Nossums first buy a piece of property that has the potential to add more bedrooms. This means the property has extra spaces that could be converted into a bedroom (e.g., a garage, a basement, a sunroom, etc.). By adding more bedrooms, they can increase the property's value and make what may have been an average single-family, single-rent property into a multi-tenant, multi-rent portfolio powerhouse.

The next step is to use the property as a rent-by-room house for a few years. This means furnishing the property as needed, marketing the property to potential tenants looking for a rent-by-room living situation, vetting tenants, creating and signing a lease, self-managing the property, taking care of ongoing maintenance, fielding tenant questions, and all of the other important responsibilities that come with being a landlord.

After a few years, the Nossums evaluate the property to determine if their strategy is serving the property. They look at comps in the area and determine the property's highest and best use. If flipping it back into a high-quality SFH makes the most sense, then they do that. If selling it as a turnkey rent-by-room house makes the most sense, then they continue using that strategy. They look at each of the different exit strategies and then go down the path that gives them the highest ROI.

One of the biggest perks of the rent-by-room strategy is the cash flow. The Nossums have some properties that make over $11,000 per month using this strategy! And bonus: The property gets the opportunity to appreciate, just like an SFH.

Rental Strategies Comparison Table

How does the rent-by-room strategy compare to the other rental models we talked about in the last chapter?

Let's break it down with a real-world example: a four-bedroom SFH in Bellevue, Washington. As a traditional long-term rental, you'd likely have one tenant or a couple leasing the whole home for around $3,500/month. If you switch to a medium-term rental model—think traveling nurses or corporate stays—you could rent out individual furnished rooms for higher rates. Altogether, you might bring in around $5,000/month.

Go the STR route, and you're looking at nightly stays—say $250 per night. That could bring in about $7,500/month, assuming full occupancy.

Now here's where things get interesting: Using the rent-by-room strategy, each bedroom could go for $1,000/month. With four bedrooms, that's $4,000/month—already beating your long-term option.

But let's say you get creative. Maybe the home has some underused space—a garage, bonus room, or an unfinished basement ripe for conversion. You carve out five extra bedrooms, bringing your total to nine. Rent each at $1,000/month and now you're grossing $9,000/month.

Talk about maximizing potential! This strategy isn't just flexible; it can be a serious cash flow engine when done right.

Rental Strategy	Monthly Rent
Long-term rental (4-bedroom)	$3,500
Medium-term rental (4-bedroom)	$5,000
Short-term rental (4-bedroom)	$7,500
Rent-by-room (4-bedroom)	$4,000
Rent-by-room (9-bedroom, optimized)	$9,000

The Challenges of Rent-by-Room

No investment opportunity is perfect, and this strategy comes with its own challenges.

One challenge investors face with this strategy is the added complexity of management. Unlike a typical single-family long-term rental, you need to find and screen multiple tenants and provide individual leases for each. However, there is a chance that these tenants stay for a year or more, which is much less of a lift than medium- or short-term rentals in terms of turnover.

Additionally, certain items in the home—like washing machines, dryers, locks, keypads, cabinets, and floors—tend to experience more wear and tear, requiring more frequent repairs. As a result, it can be difficult to find a property manager willing to fully handle the rent-by-room approach. You can also use proactive measures against this wear and tear by installing durable floors and cabinets and investing in quality appliances.

Another potential issue is parking. If your tenants own cars, parking can become a concern, especially as more vehicles taking up street parking may frustrate neighbors. You can get creative when establishing parking spaces for your property, communicate with your neighbors about the use of the property for several tenants, or proactively seek out properties with ample room for parking (garages—assuming you won't convert this into a bedroom, a corner lot, etc.).

It's essential to communicate to your tenants that neighbors appreciate curb appeal and a tidy home. While you may not have neighborhood association rules governing this, encourage tenants to keep the yard free of trash and excessive bikes to maintain a positive appearance. Set clear expectations from the beginning to prevent any petty complaints down the line.

The biggest concern for most investors with this strategy is potential disputes between tenants. A great way to minimize conflict is by renting to a group of friends or college students who already know each other. Disputes are far less likely when tenants have a preexisting relationship. Another effective tactic is establishing house rules. Having clear guidelines helps maintain order and prevent conflicts. You can create a "mission statement" around key values like security, respect, comfort, and community, so everyone understands expectations and boundaries.

Consider placing a corkboard near the front door or in a central area to display this statement. The board can also be used for announcements, weekly chores, bills, documents that need signatures, house information like Wi-Fi codes, or even social events.

Getting Started with Rent-by-Room

Not sure where to start? Here are some of the basic principles many rent-by-room operators find helpful.

- **Utilities:** The landlord (that's you) pays utilities, and tenants pay a monthly flat fee, thus preventing usage disputes.
- **Security:** Keypad codes are used on exterior doors. Additionally, bedrooms are locked with individual keys. Roommates aren't allowed to enter a bedroom space without permission of that tenant.
- **Common areas:** Shared living spaces like the living room and kitchen are for everyone, so roommates shouldn't take over one of these spaces without asking permission from their roommates. Adding furniture or decor to the space or having a big gathering in the common area should be

preceded by a whole-house discussion. It is also worth noting that everything in the common areas becomes property of the common area and thus all the tenants. To avoid trouble, expensive personal items should be kept in personal bedrooms.

- **Animals:** Pets are typically not allowed. If someone has an animal, the whole house must approve, and the pet must stay in its owner's private room or go with the owner when they leave the house. Pets can be outside in the yard, but the owner must stay with it. If a tenant has animal allergies, the pet must stay in a bedroom and is not allowed in the common areas.

- **Guests:** Guest usage can vary based on owner preferences and should be clearly outlined in the lease. For example, guests are allowed to sleep over for X number of nights. This prevents a situation in which significant others or family members just move in without proper documentation and payment.

- **Noise:** Remind tenants to keep noise levels reasonable and respectful for roommates. Post quiet hours in the lease, for example 11 p.m. to 8 a.m.

- **Communication:** Encourage your tenants to ask permission for things and situations that might affect other roommates. Examples might include long meal-prep sessions, living room dominance for an extended period of time, or having friends over. Clearly communicating this information will help decrease daily annoyances that can build up to larger disputes. If there is a dispute, ask roommates to have a respectful conversation with each other in private before getting the landlord involved. Encourage calm and clear communication. If this doesn't resolve the issue, they can then ask another housemate for assistance and discuss again. Finally, if they are still in dispute, the property manager can step in as a mediator.

Pro tip: Add all tenants to a single text chain to create an easy opportunity for communication with the landlord and/or property manager and also create a channel for general announcements, repair requests/timelines, etc.

- **Chore schedule:** All tenants should participate in housecleaning responsibilities. This includes both inside and outside chores (unless the landlord or property manager takes care of tasks like lawn mowing and snow removal). There are a wide variety of systems, (weekly chore rotations, a chore wheel, etc.) but no matter the system, everyone needs to be involved. Or, if none of the tenants want to clean, they can decide together to hire a cleaning individual to come on a regular basis to clean the residence. Keeping a clean house and yard will prevent unnecessary damage and will also keep neighbors happy, hopefully circumventing any tension they feel about you using the property as a rental.

I've created a "Rent-by-Room Self-Assessment Quiz" that you can take to determine if this is the right strategy for you. You can find it at www.BiggerPockets.com/ROIBookBonus.

Additional Challenges to Consider for a Successful Rent-by-Room Strategy

The challenges listed above are mostly about managing the space and the tenants. But as a landlord with this kind of rental, there are also larger responsibilities to address.

- **Liability concerns:** As a landlord, you may be liable for accidents or injuries occurring on the property. Ensure you have adequate insurance coverage.
- **Local zoning and regulations:** Research local zoning laws and regulations regarding rent-by-room arrangements. Ensure compliance to avoid fines or penalties.
- **Property insurance:** Review your property insurance policy to ensure it covers rent-by-room arrangements and multiple tenants.

- **Tax implications:** Consult with a tax professional to understand the tax implications of rent-by-room arrangements, including potential deductions and liabilities.
- **Tenant screening:** Develop a thorough tenant screening process to ensure you're renting to reliable, responsible tenants.
- **Emergency preparedness:** Develop a plan for handling emergencies, such as natural disasters or unexpected repairs.
- **Recordkeeping:** Maintain accurate records of rent payments, leases, and communication with tenants.
- **Compliance with fair housing laws:** Be sure to follow fair housing laws and regulations to avoid discrimination claims.

By understanding these potential challenges, you can better prepare yourself for the responsibilities and opportunities associated with a rent-by-room strategy.

Which Properties Are Prime for Rent-by-Room?

Once you've decided to explore this option, the next step is choosing a property. This strategy can work well in both expensive markets and affordable markets. To determine if your market has these types of properties, I'd suggest Googling "room for rent in [city/neighborhood]." You can also use the following methods for finding these properties:

- **Online room rental platforms:** Websites like Roomster, Hotpads, SpareRoom, and even Zillow and Airbnb specialize in room rentals and offer a wide range of options. You can filter your search by location, price, and amenities.
- **Real estate agents:** Let your agents know that you are looking for properties with six to nine bedrooms or larger homes that have the ability to add more rooms. They can help you find suitable properties and even manage the rental process.
- **Local classifieds:** Check local online classifieds like Craigslist or Facebook Marketplace for room rental listings. You can also post your own ad specifying what you're looking for.

- **Neighborhood search:** Drive around neighborhoods you're interested in and look for "room for rent" signs. You can also talk to local residents or property managers to find out about available rooms.
- **Room rental apps:** Apps like Bungalow offer a platform for finding and renting rooms in shared houses. They often include features like roommate matching and utility billing.

Educate yourself on the possibilities of this option in your area by checking out the types of rooms and properties currently available and also the average monthly rental rates.

Next, you'll search for properties like you would any deal. You'll be looking for an SFH that meets your criteria for a rent-by-room property.

The key to being successful with this strategy is optimizing a house for this particular type of usage. If you feel comfortable with a rehab, then you can look for properties where the space isn't currently being used to its full potential. Maybe there are multiple living rooms, an unfinished basement, an unused attic, a garage, a massive walk-in closet, or a recreation room. By reimagining and reconfiguring the space in a home, you can take it from three bedrooms to five. Or seven!

To be clear, I am not suggesting that you should remove all common areas and convert them to bedrooms, nor that you should create new bedrooms that are tiny and cramped just because you can. You want to look for workable ways to use the space you have, not just cram as many rooms into the building as possible. But you'll likely be surprised at how easily can add a couple bedrooms to your existing space.

> **Awesome Nossum advice:** "In our opinion, the optimal number of bedrooms is between six and nine. The goal is to have a three-to-one ratio on bathrooms so you can have three people or fewer sharing each bathroom. If you find a seven-bedroom house that only has one bathroom, you know that you will need to find space for at least one more bathroom, if not two."

The best properties for this strategy have a big footprint with a lot of bedrooms and bathrooms or a lot of underutilized space: for example, a formal living room or dining room that can be turned into bedrooms. Homes that have high ceilings, good-sized rooms, and nice common areas are the best finds, but if you can't find something perfect from the start, don't be afraid to get creative when looking to add new, decently sized bedrooms and bathrooms. You can invite a contractor to join you for a walk-through and help determine the best changes to make and estimate the cost. Often, if you are just adding walls and a closet/door, the project won't be too extreme or expensive and will be worth the extra rent you can earn.

On the other hand, completing a large-scale remodel that finishes off a previously unused space can be a larger cost to incur but also has the potential to create a large impact on your monthly cash flow and your property value over time. One such option is to add dormers to the attic to make bedrooms there viable. Other options can include finishing basements and building out extensions into unused backyard space.

A dormer is a structural element that projects from a sloping roof, typically to provide additional space, light, and ventilation to a room. It can add natural light through installed windows; increase space by providing additional headroom, floor space, or storage; and enhance ventilation through vents or windows. Dormers come in various types, including gabled, shed, eyebrow, and hipped, and can be used in different architectural styles, making them a popular feature in homes with sloping roofs.

To evaluate a deal for potential profit, you need to count the number of existing bedrooms. Then, look at what rooms rent for in your area. Next, multiply the number of bedrooms by the rental rate to arrive at the total of your monthly income. Finally, take the rent minus the potential mortgage of the property and that will be your cash flow. Of course, you will have considerations like maintenance to consider, but these basic calculations will give you a ballpark figure of what you can stand to earn.

To test the waters with the rent-by-room strategy, consider posting an ad for a single room online and gauging the response. Start small by renting out only one or two rooms in a single house to refine your management strategy and assess local demand. This approach allows you to test your pricing and advertising strategy, develop a tenant screening process, and hone your property management skills before scaling up your investment.

Case Study: A Real-Life Example of Rent-by-Room Success

Let's take a look at a case study from Shannon and Christian. They purchased an SFH in a desirable and increasingly appreciating area of Seattle for $845,000. The median price point for a Seattle home is around $842,068, with a 4 percent year-over-year increase.

Originally the house consisted of four bedrooms and one bathroom and contained an open attic space and an unfinished basement. By maximizing the usage of the attic, converting the garage, and finishing the basement, Shannon and Christian were able to turn this house into a nine-bedroom, three-bathroom rent-by-room property—with a laundry room in the basement to boot!

The renovation process took about seven months to complete. To fund this deal, they decided to work with a partner, a single guy who chose to live with the tenants in the house for a year, allowing them to get owner-occupied financing—a smart move that allowed them to take advantage of a very low interest rate, maximizing their ROI even faster. Their partner moved into the portion of the house that wasn't under construction, and once the renovation was complete, they rented out the other eight rooms. The house now makes $8,000 per month in rent.

The cherry on top of this deal was that the house was situated on an alley and had a sizable backyard. The tenants of the original house were not using the outside space, so the Nossums ended up building an ADU in the underutilized area. They opted for a detached unit and built a 1,300-square-foot SFH with three bedrooms and two bathrooms. Their total cost for the ADU was $400,000, and they sold it for $765,000—a huge profit gained on what had previously been an unused patch of grass.

What does this mean for you? Here are some key takeaways for each of our five characters. Look for the one you identify with most and then take action.

NEW-TO-THE-GAME NOAH

As a newcomer to real estate investing, you're in luck! Rent-by-room is an excellent strategy for first-time investors like yourself. Here's why:

- Accessible: Low barriers to entry make it easy to get started
- Low risk: Spread risk across multiple tenants and income streams
- Maximized returns: Potential for higher returns compared to traditional rental strategies
- Minimal up-front investment: Lower up-front costs make it more affordable
- Strong cash flow potential: Regular income from multiple tenants

Rent-by-room is an excellent way to dip your toes into real estate investing. With its potential for strong cash flow and maximized returns, it's definitely worth considering as you start your investing journey.

ACTIVE ALEX

As an experienced landlord, you're likely looking for ways to optimize your rental properties. Rent-by-room offers:

- Increased cash flow: Higher revenue potential without the high turnover rates of STRs
- Flexibility with exit strategies: Easily adjust your investment approach as market conditions or your goals change

By incorporating rent-by-room into your existing portfolio, you can:

- Enhance your overall cash flow.
- Reduce reliance on single tenants or leases.
- Maintain adaptability in a changing market.

💡 PIVOT PEYTON

Ready to pivot from flipping or traditional rentals? Rent-by-room offers:

- Steady income stream: Reliable cash flow to support your transition
- Repurposing SFHs: Breathe new life into existing properties in high-demand areas
- Flexibility and options: Easily adapt to changing market conditions or explore new investment opportunities

By transitioning to rent-by-room, you can:

- Diversify your income streams.
- Reduce reliance on a single investment strategy.
- Unlock new opportunities for growth and profitability.

💼 SEASONED-INVESTOR SAM

As a seasoned investor, you're likely seeking strategies to enhance your portfolio's performance. Rent-by-room offers:

- Diversification: Spread investments across multiple properties and tenants
- Risk mitigation: Reduce reliance on single tenants or properties
- Optimization of underutilized properties: Maximize profitability from existing assets
- Efficient management: Minimal increase in management demands

By incorporating rent-by-room into your portfolio, you can:

- Enhance overall returns.
- Reduce vulnerability to market fluctuations.
- Unlock hidden value in underutilized properties.

As a seasoned investor focused on long-term wealth-building, you'll appreciate how rent-by- room:

- Generates strong monthly cash flow: Consistent income to support your financial goals
- Offers appreciation potential: Properties can increase in value over time
- Provides multiple exit options: Flexibility to sell, refinance, or repurpose properties as needed

By incorporating rent-by-room into your long-term strategy, you can:

- Create a steady stream of passive income.
- Build lasting wealth through property appreciation.
- Maintain flexibility to adapt to changing market conditions.

Conclusion: Has Rent-by-Room Earned a Spot in Your Investment Portfolio?

Rent-by-room offers investors a unique strategy to generate substantial cash flow while building property value. By thoughtfully optimizing spaces, you can transform an average property into a high-performing investment—especially if you target markets near universities, hospitals, and airports. This approach not only provides consistent income and appreciation but also creates affordable housing options for young professionals and students. Whether you're seeking a low-drama investment with flexible management or want to maximize your property's potential, the rent-by-room strategy offers a compelling pathway to real estate success.

Chapter 5

Caring for the Future— The Lucrative World of Assisted Living

During my years in real estate investing, I stumbled upon a unique gem: the adult family home (AFH) model. This distinctive investment opportunity beckoned to a diverse group of investors, each with their own motivations. For private investors, the AFH model promised high returns (when compared to long-term or STR strategies) while providing consistent (and predictable) income—a tantalizing prospect for those seeking to grow their wealth. Experienced investors looking to diversify their portfolios found the AFH model an attractive addition to their investment mix. Meanwhile, social impact investors were drawn to the AFH model's potential to generate not only financial returns but also a positive difference in the lives of others.

Why Adult Family Homes?

The United States is experiencing a significant demographic shift, with approximately 10,000 people turning 65 every day.[5] This aging population creates a growing demand for senior housing, particularly for personalized and intimate care settings. AFHs offer a unique opportunity for real estate investors to capitalize on this investing opportunity while making a positive impact on their communities.

The growing demand for senior housing presents a unique opportunity for real estate investors through AFHs. AFHs are licensed residential homes providing care for up to six unrelated adults (or more, in some states). These homes offer a comprehensive range of services, including room, board, laundry, supervision, and assistance with daily living and personal care, with some also providing specialized care

---

[5]   Nela Richardson, "The Age of Work," ADP Research, January 27, 2025, https://www.adpresearch.com/the-age-of-work/.

for individuals with mental health issues, developmental disabilities, or dementia.

By providing personalized care in a homelike setting, AFHs offer a more intimate and comfortable alternative to traditional care facilities, allowing seniors to age in a space within their familiar neighborhoods. AFHs offer elderly individuals the perfect balance of independence and support, making them an attractive investment opportunity for real estate investors. Moreover, AFHs create local employment opportunities by requiring caregivers, supervisors, and support staff, thereby fostering job creation and economic growth. The final, appealing piece of choosing to invest in an AFH is that they are considered relatively low risk investments due to their stable and predictable income streams. This stability stems from long-term lease agreements with health care operators, providing a consistent flow of rental income. Additionally, the demand for health care services tends to be recession resistant, reducing the likelihood of vacancy or payment disruptions. As a result, AFHs offer a more secure investment option compared to other real estate investments that may be more susceptible to market fluctuations.

Investing in AFHs offers a unique combination of financial returns and social responsibility, making them a valuable addition to any real estate investment portfolio.

AFHs vs. ALFs: Uncovering the Key Differences in Elder Care Investing

When considering senior care options, two options are AFHs and assisted living facilities (ALFs).

Local laws will determine which type of care facility is an option in your state. Check your state's department of social and health services website to learn which type is available to you.

Here are the key differences between AFHs and ALFs.

Size and Setting
- **AFHs:** Smaller, residential properties with a maximum of six to eight residents, providing a personalized and homelike setting

- **ALFs:** Larger, apartment-style communities with one hundred-plus residents, offering a more clinical approach to care

Level of Care
- **AFHs:** Provide individualized care and attention to each resident
- **ALFs:** Offer varying levels of care, including clinical services, to a larger number of residents

Overall Experience
- **AFHs:** Emphasize a family-like atmosphere, promoting social interaction and community engagement
- **ALFs:** Focus on providing a range of services and amenities, with a more institutional feel

The Longevity Advantage: How Adult Family Homes Can Secure Your Financial Future

Research has consistently shown that seniors who reside in private homes, such as AFHs, tend to live longer than those in nursing homes. This phenomenon can be attributed to several factors.

- **Personalized care:** AFHs provide a more intimate and personalized care setting, where residents receive tailored attention and support. This focused care enables residents to thrive and live longer.
- **Homelike environment:** Private homes offer a warm, familiar, and comforting atmosphere, which helps reduce stress and promotes a sense of belonging. This homelike environment can contribute to a longer and healthier life.
- **Social interaction:** AFHs typically have a smaller resident-to-caregiver ratio, facilitating meaningful social interactions and relationships. Social engagement is a critical factor in promoting mental and physical well-being, leading to a longer lifespan.
- **Nutrition and meal preparation:** In AFHs, meals are often prepared in a home kitchen, allowing for more nutritious and personalized meal planning. A balanced diet is essential for maintaining health and longevity.

- **Reduced risk of infections:** Nursing homes can be breeding grounds for infections, which can be life-threatening for seniors. AFHs, with their smaller resident population, reduce the risk of infection transmission.
- **Increased autonomy:** Residents in AFHs often enjoy more freedom and autonomy, enabling them to maintain their independence and sense of purpose. This autonomy can contribute to a longer and more fulfilling life.

By providing a unique blend of personalized care, social interaction, and homelike environment, AFHs can help seniors live longer, healthier, and happier lives.

Two Paths to Profit: Exploring the Landlord and Owner-Operator Models for AFH Investing

AFHs offer two distinct options for investors: the landlord model and the owner-operator model. Let's take a look at both.

Option 1: The Landlord Model

In this approach, you, as the investor, own the property but lease it to an experienced operator who manages the day-to-day operations. This partnership can bring numerous benefits, including access to experienced professionals with a deep understanding of the AFH industry.

This partnership can also reduce risk, as the operator takes on the responsibility of managing the home. Additionally, the operator's expertise can optimize the home's performance, leading to increased profitability. By partnering with a qualified operator, you can create a win-win situation, where both parties benefit from the arrangement.

The operator runs the AFH, providing care and services to residents, and pays the owner/investor a monthly rent that is significantly higher than a traditional long-term lease. By leasing the property to an AFH operator, the owner can enjoy a steady stream of passive income through regular rent payments, all without being directly involved in the day-to-day operations. Additionally, this arrangement allows the owner-investor to transfer operational risks to the operator, thereby minimizing the exposure to potential liabilities, while still maintaining ownership and control of the property.

- **Monthly rent:** With an AFH lease, you can earn higher monthly rent compared to traditional long-term leases. For instance, a six-bedroom SFH might fetch around $7,000 per month in a traditional lease, but an AFH operator might pay $9,000 per month. This premium rent is possible because AFH operators run a business in the home, generating revenue that enables them to pay more, making it an attractive option for landlords.
- **Lease term:** The operator signs a lease for five to seven years, providing a stable and predictable income stream. Due to the required safety and medical upgrades the property will require, it doesn't make sense unless it's a long lease—usually five-plus years.
- **Triple net (NNN) lease:** The operator is responsible for paying all operating expenses, including property taxes, insurance, and maintenance.

> What is a NNN lease? A triple net (NNN) lease is a type of rental agreement where the tenant pays all operating expenses, including property taxes, insurance, and maintenance, in addition to the base rent. This arrangement provides landlords with predictable income, reduced financial risk, and increased cash flow, as the tenant assumes responsibility for all expenses.

To find a qualified operator, it's essential to connect with the right networks. Start by reaching out to state departments of social services or aging, as well as local aging facilities, such as senior centers or Area Agencies on Aging.

Option 2: The Owner-Operator Model

In this model, the investor participates in an AFH as both the landlord and operator, owning the property and running the business themself. Such an investor gains increased control over the day-to-day operations, care, and services provided, allowing them to make decisions that align with their vision and values. This hands-on approach also offers the potential for higher returns, as it eliminates the need to share profits with a separate operator. Plus, being directly involved in the lives of residents can be incredibly rewarding, providing a sense of fulfillment and purpose that comes from making a positive impact on their community.

- **Monthly revenue:** Revenue is generated from the residents' monthly payments. This is calculated by taking the average revenue per resident and multiplying it by the number of residents.
- **Expenses:** The investor/owner-operator is responsible for paying all operating expenses, including property taxes, insurance, maintenance, staffing, and care services.
- **Profit:** The profit is the difference between your monthly revenue and expenses. In the owner-operator model, your profit is higher because you don't have to pay a landlord leasing fee. (However, more profit *does* equal more work in this case.)

As a landlord investing in an AFH, it's crucial to consider the potential downsides. Here are some key challenges to be aware of.

- **Regulatory compliance:** AFHs are subject to specific zoning and regulatory requirements, which can vary by jurisdiction. Ensuring your property meets these requirements is essential to avoid fines, penalties, or even forced closure. Research local regulations and consult with experts to ensure compliance.
- **Increased wear and tear:** With multiple residents living in a single property, AFHs can lead to increased wear and tear on the facility. This may result in higher maintenance costs, including repairs to fixtures, appliances, and structural elements. Factor these potential costs into your financial projections to ensure you're prepared.
- **Neighborhood concerns:** Some neighborhoods might object to AFH facilities due to concerns about traffic, noise, or other disruptions. This could lead to community pushback, potential litigation, or even changes to local regulations. It's essential to gauge community sentiment and address concerns proactively to minimize potential issues.
- **Liability and risk:** As a landlord, you may face increased liability risks associated with AFH operations. Ensure you

have adequate insurance coverage, and consider working with an experienced AFH operator to mitigate potential risks.

By carefully weighing these potential drawbacks against the benefits, you can make an informed decision about investing in an AFH and develop strategies to mitigate potential challenges.

Comparison Chart

Now that we've described both paths, let's compare the two.

Rental Scenario	The Landlord Model (Leasing to AFH Operator)	The Owner-Operator Model
Monthly rent	Operator pays	Owner saves rent (paid to self)
Lease term	5–7 years	N/A
NNN lease (taxes, insurance, utilities)	Operator pays	Owner pays
Mortgage	Landlord pays	Owner pays
Expenses (maintenance, staffing, and care services)	Operator pays	Owner pays

Ultimately, the choice between these two options depends on a few specific criteria.

- **Investment goals.** Are you looking for passive income with minimal involvement, or do you prefer a more hands-on approach, where you can be directly involved in the business operations? Your investment goals will significantly influence which model is more suitable for you.
- **Risk tolerance.** Assess your comfort level with operational risks such as staffing challenges, regulatory compliance, and resident care issues. If you're risk averse, transferring these risks to an experienced operator might be preferable. Conversely, if you're comfortable managing these risks, the operator model might offer greater potential returns.

- **Expertise and resources.** Do you have the necessary experience and resources to operate an AFH successfully? Operating an AFH successfully requires a unique blend of caregiving expertise, business acumen, and regulatory knowledge. You'll need experience in caring for seniors or adults with disabilities, as well as the ability to manage staff, finances, and licensing requirements. Additionally, securing sufficient funding for start-up costs, staffing, and ongoing expenses is crucial. If you lack the necessary expertise or resources, it may be wise to consider partnering with experienced professionals or exploring alternative investment models that better align with your strengths and capabilities.

As you explore investment opportunities, remember that one size doesn't fit all, and it's essential to find the right fit for your unique situation. To determine if an AFH is right for you, consider whether it aligns with your investment goals and risk tolerance, is compatible with your local market and real estate landscape, is feasible within your budget and financial resources, and suits your schedule and management style. If these characteristics resonate with you, an AFH might be the lucrative opportunity you've been searching for.

The Social and Financial Benefits of Adult Family Homes

One of the simplest ways to enter this market is by purchasing existing AFHs. By buying an existing AFH, you can reduce the need for costly renovations, such as making the home ADA accessible or adding fire sprinklers.

- **Research local regulations:** Familiarize yourself with state and local laws governing AFHs. Understand licensing requirements, zoning regulations, and health department standards. A critical aspect of local regulations is the maximum number of bedrooms allowed in a home. This varies significantly from state to state.
- **Networking:** Connect with local real estate agents, care home administrators, and health care professionals. They

can provide valuable insights and leads on potential AFH properties. Some brokers specialize in AFH sales.

- **Facebook:** There are dozens of Facebook groups dedicated to AFHs, and you can look them up by city or state. You can find homes, caregivers, operators, and whole communities dedicated to senior living.
- **Drive-by searches:** Physically drive through neighborhoods and search for care homes or properties with conversion potential. A key indicator to look out for is the presence of large signs outside homes clearly stating they are an AFH. These signs can be a dead giveaway that the property is already operating as an AFH or has the potential to be converted into one.

Ideal Properties for Adult Family Homes

If you are unable to find an existing AFH to purchase, you can always find a property to convert into an AFH. To ensure you're well equipped to find and evaluate the perfect properties, I'll share my top tips and insights on what to look for in an AFH property.

When searching for a property to convert into an AFH, there are a variety of property styles that can work. As you search, consider the following:

- **SFHs:** Existing or newly built homes in residential areas
- **Small multiunit properties:** Duplexes, triplexes, or small apartment buildings
- **Properties in residential areas:** Homes in quiet neighborhoods with easy access to community amenities

Crucial Considerations: What to Look for in an AFH Property

Once you've identified a potential property, it's essential to conduct a thorough evaluation to determine its suitability for an AFH.

- **Size and layout:** A large home with three to six bedrooms, an open floor plan, and wheelchair accessibility
- **Location:** Proximity to community amenities, public transportation, and health care services

- **Age and condition:** Newer homes may be more expensive, while older homes may require renovation
- **Lot size:** A large lot provides ample outdoor space for residents
- **Accessibility and safety features:** Wide doorways, ramps, elevators (depending on the property type—this may be more suited for an ALF), grab bars, and emergency call systems

Property Characteristics: The Must-Haves for a Successful AFH

Specifically, on my AFH property wish list are these characteristics:

- **Number of bedrooms:** three to six bedrooms
- **Square footage:** Minimum 1,500–2,000 square feet
- **Bathrooms:** At least two to three bathrooms with walk-in showers and grab bars
- **Parking and outdoor spaces:** Ample parking and secure outdoor areas

The Financial Aspects of Adult Family Homes

There are several ways to finance this strategy. It's important that you understand what each of those are. Based on the option you choose, there will be additional information you need to know. The following is a brief synopsis of the different strategies you can use to finance your property. (You can find more information about funding AFHs on episode #710 of the *BiggerPockets Real Estate* podcast at www.BiggerPockets/BookRealEstatePodcast.)

- **Conventional loans:** Explore conventional loan options from banks, credit unions, or mortgage companies. These loans typically require a significant down payment and good credit.
- **Specialized lenders:** Look for lenders specializing in health care or senior housing financing. These lenders may offer more favorable terms and competitive interest rates.
- **Small Business Administration (SBA) loans:** Consider SBA loans, which can provide favorable terms, such as lower down payments and longer repayment periods.

- **Private money lenders:** Private money lenders may offer short-term, high-interest loans for AFH acquisitions or renovations.
- **Investor partnerships:** Collaborate with investors or partners to share the financial burden and risks associated with AFH ownership.
- **Government incentives:** Research government programs, such as Medicaid or VA benefits, that can provide financial support for AFH operations.

Avoiding Common Pitfalls in AFH Investing

Each state, city, and county has different rules and regulations for operating an AFH. You'll want to do your due diligence to ensure that you are prepared to own and operate an AFH. The rules are always changing. Please make sure to research the most up-to-date information.

Here are some items to consider in your research process.

- **Local regulations and zoning:** Before investing in an AFH, it's crucial to ensure the property meets specific local regulations and zoning requirements. These may include compliance with building codes, such as fire safety standards and emergency exit routes, as well as room specifications like minimum bedroom size and window height. Additionally, properties must meet accessibility standards for residents with disabilities and adhere to health and safety standards for sanitation and hygiene. Verifying zoning restrictions and obtaining necessary permits or variances is also essential. Failure to comply with these regulations can result in fines, penalties, or even closure of the AFH.
- **Licensing and certification:** AFHs require specific licenses and certifications to operate, typically obtained from the state's department of health or social services. These licenses ensure AFHs meet minimum standards for resident care, safety, and well-being. To maintain licensure, AFHs must undergo regular inspections and comply with ongoing requirements, such as staff training and certification. By obtaining and maintaining necessary

licenses and certifications, AFH operators demonstrate their commitment to providing high-quality care and services to residents.

- **Market demand and competition:** It is crucial to research local market demand and competition. This involves analyzing demographic trends, population growth, and the need for senior care services in the area, as well as identifying existing AFHs, their occupancy rates, and services offered. By evaluating the competitive landscape and identifying gaps in services or unmet needs, investors can make informed decisions and potentially capitalize on opportunities for success in the market.

- **Property condition and modifications:** It is essential to consider the property's condition and potential modifications needed to meet resident needs and regulatory requirements. This may involve installing accessibility features like ramps and wheelchair-accessible bathrooms, safety features such as handrails and emergency alert systems, and converting rooms to meet licensing standards. Assessing the property's condition and modification costs helps investors determine the feasibility and potential ROI, ensuring the property can be safely and effectively operated as an AFH.

- **Financing options and costs:** Explore financing options and calculate associated costs. This includes evaluating mortgage options, such as conventional loans or government-backed loans, and determining down payment requirements. Additionally, investors must calculate ongoing operating costs, including staffing, utilities, and maintenance, to ensure the financial sustainability of the AFH. Understanding potential funding sources, like Medicaid or private pay, can also help investors make informed decisions and develop a comprehensive financial plan

- **Staffing and caregiver qualifications:** AFHs require caregivers who meet specific state and local qualifications to ensure quality care for residents. Caregivers typically need to complete state-mandated training programs, obtain certifications such as CNA or medication management, and pass background checks to guarantee resident safety.

Additionally, AFHs must adhere to staffing ratios to provide adequate care and supervision. By meeting these qualifications, caregivers can provide compassionate and competent care, and AFH operators can maintain licensure and build trust with residents and their families.

- **Resident needs and services:** Consider the specific needs and services required by residents. This may include providing assistance with daily living activities like bathing, dressing, and medication management, as well as offering specialized care for residents with dementia, Alzheimer's, or other conditions. Additionally, AFHs may need to provide access to therapeutic services like physical, occupational, or speech therapy, and organize social activities to promote resident engagement and well-being. By tailoring services to meet individual needs, AFHs can enhance residents' quality of life.

Moving Forward with Confidence in AFH Investing

Taking on any investment is a big deal, but this one, especially, where you are potentially taking responsibility for the living situations of several other people, is a really big deal. I want to send you on your way from this chapter with some things to think about. Hopefully these questions will help you reflect and decide if an AFH is the right investment strategy for you.

NEW-TO-THE-GAME NOAH

Traits: Curious, cautious, eager to learn, focused on stable income

AFH Fit: Noah is intrigued by the reliable cash flow AFHs can offer but would likely start with the landlord model to avoid operational complexity.

Q: What kind of license or regulation is required to own an AFH in my area?
A: Each state has different rules—check with your Department of Social or Health Services to understand zoning, licensing, and occupancy limits.

Q: How much more rent can I really expect from an AFH compared to a regular long-term rental?
A: Often 20–40 percent more. For example, a home that rents for $7,000 traditionally might lease to an AFH operator for $9,000+ monthly.

Q: Who takes care of the residents—do I have to be involved in the caregiving side?
A: Not with the landlord model. The operator hires caregivers and manages all care services.

Q: What are the up-front costs to buy or convert a property into an AFH?
A: Costs vary, but budget for ADA upgrades, fire sprinklers, extra bathrooms, and compliance items—often $50,000–$150,000.

Q: How do I find and vet a reliable AFH operator?
A: Start with senior care associations, state registries, Facebook groups, and referrals from senior centers or brokers specializing in AFHs.

ACTIVE ALEX

Traits: Creative, hands-on, passionate about environments that foster connection

AFH Fit: Alex thrives in designing intentional spaces. An AFH allows for purpose-driven renovations and meaningful resident interaction through thoughtful layout and atmosphere.

Q: Am I ready to become an operator, or should I lease the property to someone who can run the AFH?
A: Your hands-on nature suits being both landlord and operator, but it's important to assess if you want to juggle both roles. If you decide to pursue this route, I would not be wishy-washy about which path (owner or owner-operator) you will take. Your indecision will lead to miscommunication and mistakes that could not only be costly, but could potentially put your residents (renters) at risk.

Q: Am I ready to use my design eye to build not just beautiful spaces but better lives for seniors?

A: Your DIY skills could be useful for making modifications to meet AFH standards, but it's crucial to understand regulatory requirements associated with elderly care. Do you have this knowledge, or do you have someone you can ask to help with all that it entails to meet compliance?

Q: How much time am I willing to dedicate to daily operations?
A: Running an AFH requires active involvement, especially if you're operating the business and managing residents' care. Do you have this time currently or will you be off-loading another major task that will open space in your day-to-day operations?

Q: Can I manage the stress of compliance, staffing, and potential liability?
A: AFH operations come with high responsibility for resident safety and care, which requires focus, adaptability, and commitment. Is this a role you are ready to take on?

💡 PIVOT PEYTON

Traits: Opportunistic, analytical, thrives on reinvention and strategic pivots

AFH Fit: Peyton sees demographic trends and policy shifts as signals. With the right operator, Peyton can convert underutilized single-family rentals into AFHs for better returns.

Q: Am I ready to pivot my investment strategy to include a more specialized asset?
A: AFHs are different from traditional rental properties, requiring creative and flexible thinking for both compliance and profitability. Are you interested in investing in a niche market and the responsibilities that come along with caring for the elderly population?

Q: How can I maximize the value of the property while balancing care requirements?
A: Are you interested in applying your creative thinking skills to space usage and optimizing resident care with the desired result being both a lucrative investment and thriving living environment?

Q: Am I comfortable experimenting with a highly regulated industry?
A: AFHs require navigating licensing and operational regulations, which may be more rigid than you're used to in other investments. Are you willing to insert yourself into a niche of the real estate industry that has a stricter structure than others you may have invested in before? How will you react when a rule or regulation tells you no and has no wiggle room? Is that a place you are interested in entering willingly?

Q: How can I find opportunities in local markets with growing senior populations?
A: Your knack for identifying market trends can help you find regions with rising demand for senior housing. Is this a housing treasure hunt that sounds appealing to you?

💼 SEASONED-INVESTOR SAM

Traits: Strategic, data driven, focused on scale and stability

AFH Fit: Sam understands how AFHs fit into a balanced portfolio. The long-term leases, NNN structure, and recession-resistant income appeal to his risk-adjusted return mindset.

Q: How can I leverage my existing network to operate or partner in AFH investments?
A: With your contacts, you could consider forming partnerships with experienced operators or health care professionals. Off the top of your head, do any people come to mind you could approach about partnering with you in this endeavor? Or does someone you know have a connection? Is the idea of working with a partner on this kind of investment appealing to you?

Q: Am I ready to handle the added liability and risks that come with managing care for elderly residents?
A: You are accustomed to calculated risks, but AFHs come with unique legal and operational risks due to the nature of senior care. Is this an arena you feel emboldened to enter? What will you do to prepare yourself to be ready to handle this specific set of challenges (should they arise… and you should assume that they will rather than cross your fingers and hope for the best!).

Q: Can I scale my investments in AFHs for significant returns?
A: With the right structures in place, you could grow a portfolio of AFHs, providing both financial growth and legacy. Does that sound appealing? Is this an area that you'd like to focus your future on? The market looks favorable for you to do so, but just because you *can* doesn't mean you *should*. Do you *want* to? What is appealing about the idea of a portfolio full of AFHs?

Q: Is this a lucrative enough opportunity for the level of hands-on involvement required?
A: Given your desire for higher returns, assess if the potential earnings from AFHs align with your current investment goals. Also, consider the time investment piece of this strategy. Do the added benefits of contributing to your community outweigh the time sacrifices you may need to make?

LONG-GAME LOGAN

Traits: Risk averse, values longevity, focused on building generational wealth

AFH Fit: Logan is drawn to recession-resistant models with reliable income. AFHs—especially under the landlord model—align perfectly with Logan's preference for steady, long-term plays.

Q: Are AFHs truly recession resistant, and how has their performance held up in past downturns?
A: Yes. Health care needs remain constant, and AFHs stayed stable during the Great Recession and even through COVID.

Q: Can I invest passively while ensuring quality care and compliance from the operator?
A: Yes—with the landlord model, you remain hands-off. Vet your operator thoroughly and conduct occasional property reviews.

Q: What's the ideal lease structure to protect my cash flow for the next ten-plus years?
A: A five-to-ten-year NNN lease with annual rent increases and clear compliance clauses offers strong protection.

Q: How do I evaluate the strength and experience of an operator before signing a lease?
A: Ask for licensing history, references, financials, and occupancy track record. Look for operators with multiple successful AFHs.

Q: Will this investment allow me to leave a meaningful legacy for my family—and my community?
A: Absolutely. AFHs combine consistent cash flow with social impact—providing care, jobs, and dignity to aging adults.

Discovering AFHs was a turning point in my real estate journey. I had spent years flipping homes, building rental portfolios, and navigating the ups and downs of the market—but AFHs introduced me to something different. Something more sustainable. More meaningful. They weren't just a high cash flow asset class; they were a way to invest in people and community while still achieving strong, predictable returns.

I've seen firsthand how this model can work—whether you're leasing to an operator or running the home yourself. I've worked with investors from all walks of life who found success in AFHs, each for their own reasons. Some wanted stable, long-term income. Others wanted to be part of something with purpose. And many, like me, wanted both.

This chapter isn't just a blueprint; it's an invitation. If you're looking for a strategy that offers consistency, impact, and long-term potential, AFHs might be the missing piece in your portfolio. Ask yourself the hard questions, know your strengths, and when you're ready, take that next step with confidence. This could be one of the most fulfilling investments you ever make.

Conclusion to Part 2

As I reflect on these three operating models—various length-of-stay models, rent-by-room, and AFHs—I'm reminded of the power of flexibility in real estate investing. Discovering these options allowed me to think creatively about how to optimize my properties and achieve my financial goals. My hope is that you've gained a similar perspective and that you'll use this newfound knowledge to chart your own course, experimenting with different models until you find the perfect fit for your unique situation.

I have personally invested in short-term, long-term, and AFHs. My STR, a cozy studio apartment in Queen Anne, is a hot spot for tourists and partygoers. I've listed it on popular vacation rental platforms, and it's generating a lucrative income stream. However, managing STRs comes with its own set of challenges—from dealing with rowdy guests to handling last-minute cancellations. Despite the headaches, the extra income is worth it.

In contrast, my long-term rental in Ballard provides a steady stream of income with minimal daily management. I've rented out a two-bedroom house to a family of four, who pay their rent on time and take good care of the property. This investment gives me a sense of stability and predictability, allowing me to focus on other ventures.

But my most rewarding investment is the AFH in Shoreline, which I've leased to a compassionate and experienced operator. I'm passionate about supporting initiatives that help others, and knowing that this AFH provides a safe and supportive environment for its residents fills me with a sense of purpose. I'm confident that the operator's expertise and care will make a positive impact on the lives of the residents, and I'm proud to be a part of it by providing a suitable property for their important work.

As we close this chapter on exploring innovative real estate investment models, I'm excited for the possibilities that lie ahead. Whether you're drawn to the dynamic world of STRs, the income potential of rent-by-room, or the impact of AFHs, the key is to find the model that aligns with your vision and goals.

I hope this knowledge empowers you to think outside the box, seize new opportunities, and build a real estate portfolio that not only generates wealth but also brings fulfillment. Here's to creating a brighter financial future, one investment at a time!

PART THREE

Value Boosters

Get Ready to Supercharge Your Investments!

If, as a real estate investor, you only focus on buying and holding—you're going to miss out. To be successful in this industry, you need to recognize and pursue opportunities that will add value to your properties and help you maximize your returns. The great news for you is that there are all sorts of ways to discover and tap into that hidden value. Whether you're rolling up your sleeves to renovate a property, restructuring your financing to free up capital, or transforming a single property into multiple income streams, there are countless ways to increase a property's worth beyond market appreciation. Smart investors know that creativity and strategy can turn an average deal into an exceptional one.

As the famous entrepreneur and real estate mogul, Robert Kiyosaki, once said: "The biggest risk is not taking any risk . . . "[6]

In the following chapters, we'll explore the most effective strategies for adding value to your investments, from refinance and renovation to subdivision and exchanges. The more you understand how to enhance value, the more control you'll have over your financial future. Perhaps the best news is that no matter which character persona you've been leaning into on this *Choose Your Own Adventure* real estate journey, there are possibilities waiting for you. Let's dive into the strategies that can take your investments to the next level.

---

[6]   Robert Kiyosaki, *Rich Dad Poor Dad* (Plata Publishing, 1997).

Chapter 6

Sweat Equity Secrets to Making Big Bucks

The term "sweat equity" might sound a little intense. It might make you a little nervous, or even make your hands, well, sweaty. And that's okay! Sweat equity refers to the value-enhancing improvements generated from the sweat of one's brow. In other words, it's going to take some hard work.

Instead of investing money, sweat equity investors are investing their physical labor, their renovation knowledge, and their personal time to boost the value of a specific project or venture—in this case, the value of a property. By investing sweat equity, investors can deliberately enhance the property's condition, functionality, and aesthetic appeal, thereby increasing its value. This increase in property value resulting from targeted renovations, repairs, and improvements is known as "forced appreciation." Unlike market appreciation, which is influenced by external factors, forced appreciation is a direct result of intentional improvements and renovations made to the property.

These renovated properties can command higher rental rates, increasing cash flow and potential returns. Properties with forced appreciation are also more attractive to potential buyers, reducing marketing time and increasing the likelihood of a successful sale. Furthermore, renovation expenses can be tax deductible, providing additional financial benefits and making forced appreciation a savvy investment strategy.

If you are an Active Alex, a Pivot Peyton, or a New-to-the-Game Noah, then this chapter is likely full of adventures you're going to want to choose! (Seasoned-Investor Sams and Long-Game Logans are already well acquainted with sweat equity, but there may be some gold nuggets here for them as well.)

By leveraging sweat equity, you can improve your property's value, making it more attractive for refinancing, selling, or scaling your investment portfolio. If this sounds appealing to you, it's time to roll up your sleeves and dig in.

Calculating the Sweat Equity Advantage (No Math Degree Required!)

To better understand this concept, let's look at a real-life example.

A couple of years ago, I purchased a house in Seattle from a pair of siblings who had inherited the property from their mother. They wanted a quick sale and were willing to let it go for $200,000, despite its worth being closer to $275,000. I seized the opportunity, paying cash up front. I knew I could rent out a property like this for $1,500/month. But I wanted to do better than that.

So, to increase the property's value, I invested time and effort into cleaning and landscaping, upgrading a bathroom, and repairing kitchen cabinets and flooring.

After working on this property for four to six weeks (and spending $7,000 on updates and materials), I rented the property for $2,300/month. When I refinanced the property, it appraised for $345,000.

Without investing sweat equity, the outcome would have been vastly different.

- Rental income would have been capped at around $1,500/month, significantly lower than the $2,300/month achieved after renovations
- The property's value would have been limited to around $275,000, and potentially even considered distressed
- The lack of renovations and upkeep would have resulted in a lower appraisal value, limiting refinancing options

In contrast, the sweat equity invested in the property:

- Increased rental income by $800/month.
- Boosted the property's value by $70,000.
- Enabled a more favorable refinancing option, allowing me to recoup of the initial investment.

This scenario highlights the significant impact of sweat equity on both rental income and property value, demonstrating how a little hard work and investment can yield substantial returns.

How to Turn Elbow Grease into Cold, Hard Cash

There are a lot of different areas of a home as well as a lot of different ways you can apply the brute force of sweat equity. Take a look at the list below and consider if any of these ideas are applicable to the properties currently in your portfolio.

- **Renovations and repairs:** Focus on upgrading critical areas, such as kitchens, bathrooms, and flooring, to create a modern and desirable living space
- **Cosmetic improvements:** Enhance the property's curb appeal through landscaping, painting, and exterior renovations
- **Functional improvements:** Add value by installing new fixtures, appliances, and systems, such as HVAC and plumbing
- **Energy efficiency:** Invest in energy-efficient upgrades, like insulation, windows, and solar panels, to reduce operating costs and attract eco-conscious buyers
- **Amenities and features:** Add desirable amenities, such as a backyard patio, deck, or pool, to increase the property's appeal

The first step in this process is to decide if your property needs or could benefit from renovations and improvements. The answer is usually yes—there's almost always something that could be improved. But a more appropriate question for this situation is to ask whether the time, energy, and money spent to make that improvement will be worth it. Will your efforts provide a return on your investment? Even if your investment is only sweat equity, will your time invested be returned to you in cash?

One easy way to tell if your property can significantly benefit from added value is if it is currently underperforming. If there is a loss of rent due to vacancies, or inability to raise rents because of the condition of the property, then it is a good time to step in and identify areas that could benefit from sweat equity. There is always low-hanging fruit when it comes to increasing the value of the property. Here are a few examples:

- Update the flooring
- Update appliances
- Update finishes
- Fresh paint
- Minor restructure of floor plan (can a wall be removed/ added to update the "flow" of the property?)

You don't want to get overwhelmed by updating everything, so finding (and focusing on) the essential upgrades that will get the most bang for your buck is a great way to determine how much time, effort, and energy you'll need (and want) to spend.

For example, if I have a unit that is underperforming, I run through a premade checklist to see where there might be an area of opportunity to make upgrades. (You can download this checklist at www.BiggerPockets.com/ROIBookBonus.)

First on my list is the kitchen. I evaluate what, if any, upgrades need to be made. The kitchen is the heart of the home and one of the most important for buyers and renters when making their decisions. Ask yourself, is there enough storage space? Does the layout make sense for the unit? Are the cabinets appealing? Are there any (affordable!) finishes or hardware I could add that would make a great first impression? What about the paint color and the flooring? Basically, I'm trying to figure out some quick, easy, and *cheap* ways I can improve the kitchen and improve the performance of the unit.

Once I evaluate the kitchen, I can move on to other living spaces. I evaluate the paint, the flooring, and the lighting as well as the window treatments and doors. Once I evaluate the living spaces, I look at the bathrooms. Bathrooms can be an area for major overhaul, but small updates can massively improve the performance of your listing. Things like new cabinets, a fresh coat of paint, updated flooring, an added toilet, new hardware, additional towel racks, and linen storage can help improve your property with just a little bit of time and sweat equity.

Remember that your goal is to simply improve the performance of your property. If you're looking to flip a home, or make substantial updates with the intention to sell, my advice is going to be a little different. To get the full story on those situations, jump ahead to Chapter 10 where we discuss flipping. The goal here is to renovate with a hold-and-rent strategy in mind.

Beyond looking at your property as an individual entity, you should also consider if your property is located in an emerging neighborhood or is situated in a market with strong demand for upgraded properties. If one or both of these is true, improving the property will almost certainly lead to better tenants and higher rental rates, so renovations will be worth it.

Finally, once you decide that a property requires repairs or renovations, the next step is to figure out who is going to do that work. You might guess, based on the title of this chapter, that I'm going to suggest *you* do the work, and usually I will, but that isn't always the case. Real estate investors and even homeowners can lower the cost by doing the work themselves, but they also have the option of hiring a subcontractor to take on the work. If you take the second route and hire out the work, be warned that paying a builder or general contractor can be expensive (see Chapter 10 for more information on working with contractors). I would recommend getting multiple bids before making a selection. But if you have the skills to complete the work yourself, know that using your own time and labor is a cost-effective way to raise the final exit value of a property.

Why Renovation-Driven Appreciation Works Like Magic

By incorporating renovation-driven appreciation into your investment strategy, you can create a winning formula for forcing appreciation, generating income, and building equity. Renovated properties are often in high demand, especially in competitive markets where buyers and renters seek move-in-ready homes. Thoughtful upgrades can also evoke an emotional response, making a property more appealing and increasing the likelihood of strong offers. Well-executed renovations enhance a property's perceived value, positioning it as a more desirable option compared to outdated or neglected homes. By strategically improving a property's condition and aesthetics, you can maximize its market potential and overall ROI.

When it comes to adding value to your property through sweat equity, one of the most important decisions you'll make is whether to tackle the renovations yourself (DIY) or hire contractors to do the work. Both options have their pros and cons, which are outlined below.

Pros of DIY Sweat Equity

- **Cost savings:** By doing the work yourself, you eliminate the need to pay contractors, potentially saving a significant amount of money. You'll also save the time you would have spent finding and interviewing contractors.
- **Full control:** You have complete oversight of the quality, timeline, and execution of the project, ensuring it aligns with your vision and standards.
- **Skill development:** You gain valuable hands-on experience and improve your construction, renovation, and problem-solving skills.
- **Customization:** You can make on-the-spot adjustments and decisions, ensuring the project meets your exact preferences and requirements.
- **Pride in the work:** Completing a project yourself can provide a sense of personal accomplishment and satisfaction.

Challenges of DIY Sweat Equity

- **Time consuming:** DIY projects can take much longer than hiring professionals, especially if you're juggling multiple projects and other responsibilities.
- **Skill limitations:** If you're not an expert, you may end up taking on projects beyond your capability, which can lead to costly mistakes and potentially subpar results.
- **Physical and mental strain:** The physical labor involved can be taxing, not to mention the stress of managing a project can be overwhelming. Especially on top of work and family commitments, the project may feel (mentally and physically) like more than you can handle.
- **Legal and code compliance:** Without the knowledge of local building codes and regulations, you might overlook necessary permits or fail inspections, leading to fines or delays or, even worse, unsafe living conditions for future buyers/tenants.
- **Inconsistent results:** Since you're working alone, the final outcome may lack the consistency and refinement that professional contractors could provide with their years of honed experience.

Pros of Outsourced Sweat Equity

They are called professionals for a reason—they know what they are doing and are good at it. So it shouldn't surprise you that there are several reasons why hiring a contractor can be a great choice.

- **Expertise and experience:** Contractors bring specialized knowledge, experience, and craftsmanship to the table, ensuring high-quality work that meets industry standards.
- **Time efficiency:** Professionals can complete projects much faster than inexperienced rookies and hobbyists, helping you meet deadlines and avoid extended delays (that can cost a lot of money).
- **Access to resources:** Builders typically have faster and easier access to better tools, equipment, and materials, ensuring the job is done more efficiently and with higher-quality resources.
- **Less stress and responsibility:** With professionals handling the project, you can avoid the day-to-day stress of overseeing construction and focus on other aspects of your life or business.
- **Warranty and insurance:** Many contractors offer warranties on their work, and they're usually insured, providing peace of mind in case of accidents or issues during the project.

Challenges of Outsourced Sweat Equity

But like any this-or-that scenario, there are potential challenges involved with hiring a contractor to do work. The items on this list should receive careful attention from everyone but should especially be taken into consideration if you are capable of completing the work yourself.

- **Higher costs:** Hiring contractors can be expensive, as you're paying for both their labor and overhead costs on top of the cost of materials
- **Less control:** Outsourcing means giving up some level of control over the project's details, and you may need to rely on others to make key decisions

- **Coordination challenges:** Managing multiple contractors or subcontractors can be complex and may require extra time and effort on your part to ensure smooth communication and project progression
- **Quality variability:** Not all contractors deliver the same quality of work. Hiring the wrong builder or contractor can result in substandard results, which may not meet your expectations.
- **Potential delays:** Depending on the contractor's schedule, availability, or unforeseen issues, delays can occur, especially if the contractor has multiple project sites or you're not working with a highly reliable professional

When it comes down to it, the choice between being hands-on or outsourcing depends on your skills, time availability, and the scope of the project. If you're highly capable and have time to dedicate, being hands-on can save money and provide a sense of accomplishment. However, if you value quality, efficiency, and professional oversight, outsourcing to contractors or builders may be the better option, despite the higher cost. (I will expand on how to hire contractors and manage contractors on larger projects in Chapter 10.) Balancing both approaches, such as handling smaller tasks yourself while outsourcing major work, can also be an effective strategy.

How to Maximize Your Profits After a Successful Renovation (and Avoid the Post-Reno Blues)

Successfully completing a project and making a profit opens up several strategic avenues for leveraging the equity you've built in your property. The key is to unlock that equity in a way that fuels further investment or provides capital for other opportunities. Once you've increased the value of your property through renovation, improvements, or sweat equity, you now have several options for tapping into this new value.

Let's explore a few common ways to leverage that equity.

1. Increase Rent

After completing minor renovations and repairs, you can leverage the increased equity in your property by boosting rental income. This strategy is particularly effective when you've added value to the property through cosmetic upgrades or minor renovations. This allows you to amplify cash flow and improve profitability and enhance the property's resale value, should you decide to sell in the future.

- **Pros:** Increased cash flow and profitability can provide a significant ROI
- **Cons:** Raising rent too high can lead to increased vacancy rates, as tenants may be priced out of the market

2. Refinancing (Cash Out Refinance)
Refinancing allows you to replace your existing mortgage with a new one, pulling out cash based on the increased value. This option provides immediate access to funds without selling the property. If this sounds a bit overwhelming (or perhaps just a bit over your head), don't worry, we are going to cover it in depth in the next chapter.

- **Pros:** Access to cash, potential for lower interest rates, and no need to sell
- **Cons:** Increased debt, refinancing costs, and higher monthly payments

3. Home Equity Line of Credit (HELOC)
A HELOC lets you borrow against your property's equity, offering a revolving line of credit you can use as needed.

- **Pros:** Flexible access to funds, lower interest rates than personal loans, and interest-only payments during the draw period
- **Cons:** Variable interest rates, risk of foreclosure if payments aren't made, and limited borrowing capacity

4. Selling the Property
Selling your property outright allows you to cash in on the increased value, paying off any outstanding mortgage and keeping the profit. (Reminder that the focus of this chapter is to use sweat equity to improve the value of the home with the intent to hold and rent the property, leveraging the renovations to increase rents and attract high-quality tenants. However, if you find that the best-use case for

the property is not to rent but to sell, this is a great option. We'll discuss fix-and-flip in Chapter 10, where the intent of buying the property is to sell.)

- **Pros:** Immediate cash flow, no debt, and the potential for significant profits if the market is strong
- **Cons:** Loss of future appreciation, transaction costs (e.g., realtor fees, taxes), and market volatility

The choice between refinancing, taking out a HELOC, or selling depends on your long-term goals and financial strategy. Refinancing and HELOCs are ideal if you want to maintain ownership of the property and continue benefiting from its appreciation while accessing capital for future investments. On the other hand, selling may be a better option if you're looking for a quick return on your investment or want to exit the market entirely.

Ultimately, how you leverage the equity you've built should align with your investment goals, risk tolerance, and future plans. By understanding your options and the potential benefits as well as possible drawbacks of each, you can make a more informed decision on how best to use the value you've added to your property.

Key Takeaways and Essential Insights to Supercharge Your Investments

As we wrap up our in-depth look at sweat equity, one thing is clear: This has the potential to revolutionize real estate investing. By taking a hands-on approach and investing their own time and effort, investors can tap into a wealth-building strategy that drives significant returns, fosters long-term financial growth, and brings financial goals within reach.

📍📊 **NEW-TO-THE-GAME NOAH: START SMALL, THINK BIG**

Key takeaway: Sweat equity is an ideal entry point for new investors. By starting small—painting, landscaping, updating fixtures—Noah can build experience, increase a property's value, and improve cash flow without needing a large up-front investment.

Action items:
- Look for cosmetic fixer-uppers with functional layouts in good locations
- Learn basic home renovation skills through YouTube, DIY books, or weekend workshops
- Use a checklist to evaluate properties for quick, value-boosting upgrades

ACTIVE ALEX: RENOVATION PRIORITIZATION 101

Key takeaway: Alex can combine design flair with smart renovations to enhance both form and function. Strategic upgrades aligned with market trends will not only increase rental income but also attract better tenants.

Action items:
- Focus on high-impact aesthetic updates like backsplashes, light fixtures, and hardware
- Create a signature design style that can be replicated across multiple properties
- Use mood boards to plan value-adding renovations before starting work

PIVOT PEYTON: REASSESSING SWEAT EQUITY FOR MAXIMUM RETURNS

Key takeaway: Sweat equity offers Peyton a reliable tool for repositioning stagnant or poorly performing properties. With a flexible approach, Peyton can renovate for rent or resale based on shifting market conditions.

Action items:
- Perform a rent analysis to identify underperforming units in the portfolio
- Prioritize "low lift" updates like paint, flooring, and landscaping
- Use market comps to determine if the upgrade should support a refinance or a flip

Key takeaway: Sam can streamline renovation processes by outsourcing labor-intensive work while maintaining oversight. Sweat equity becomes a tool for scaling and repositioning portfolios, not just individual projects.

Action items:
- Create systems and standard operating procedures (SOPs) for repeat renovations across multiple properties
- Leverage equity gains from renovations to fund future investments
- Build long-term relationships with vetted contractors to reduce delays and risk

🕐 **LONG-GAME LOGAN: STRATEGIC UPGRADES FOR PASSIVE INCOME**

Key takeaway: For Logan, sweat equity should focus on durable upgrades that reduce long-term maintenance and improve tenant retention. Renovate once, hold long term, and minimize future involvement.

Action items:
- Invest in energy-efficient appliances, low-maintenance landscaping, and durable materials
- Renovate to accommodate long-term renters' needs: storage, work-from-home setups, quiet living
- Set clear criteria for what qualifies as a worthwhile improvement based on ROI and time horizon

Sweat equity isn't just about putting in hard work; it's about using your resources wisely to drive returns. Whether you're just starting out or looking to scale strategically, there's a role for sweat equity in every investor's toolbox.

Chapter 7

Refi Revival—Breathe New Life into Your Investments

There are two ways a property's value can increase over time: market appreciation and forced appreciation. While market appreciation is mostly passive, forced appreciation is truly active. I always recommend investing in both types to balance out your portfolio, but we have to start with one and then build up from there. Instead of thinking about a full portfolio, let's just think about a single piece of property.

First, we're going to look at market appreciation. Long-Game Logan, listen up, because this is going to be especially appealing for you! Market appreciation occurs when a property's value rises due to external factors, such as improvements in the local economy, housing demand, or changes in the neighborhood. This increase is typically driven by factors beyond the property owner's control, such as a booming job market, new infrastructure developments, or rising demand in the area. Market appreciation takes time and requires patience because it is often gradual and tied to broader market trends.

Active Alex, now it's your turn. Forced appreciation happens when a property owner actively improves or renovates the property to increase its value. There are lots of ways to make this happen, including making physical upgrades, such as remodeling the kitchen, adding a bathroom, enhancing curb appeal, or addressing issues like structural repairs. Forced appreciation allows the owner to directly influence the property's value, often resulting in a quicker and more noticeable increase in value compared to market appreciation. It also allows the owner to move at their own pace to achieve their desired increased value. Projects can be completed as fast as time and your budget allow or move at a leisurely pace if that is what you prefer (and have time for).

Once a property's value has increased, or appreciated, it's time to refinance. It's not a requirement, but refinancing your property can be an awesome way to access funds or improve your financial situation.

It's not typically considered a direct way to "make money" in real estate; however, refinancing can help you leverage the equity in your property to achieve specific financial goals. For example:

- If interest rates have dropped or your credit score has improved since you first purchased your property, refinancing to a lower rate can reduce your monthly mortgage payment, freeing up cash for other investments or expenses.
- A cash out refinance allows you to borrow against the equity you've built in your home, providing funds for home improvements, debt consolidation, or even investment opportunities, thus potentially increasing your wealth over time.
- Refinancing can help consolidate high-interest debts, such as credit cards, into a lower-interest mortgage, reducing overall interest payments.
- For those looking to pay off their mortgage more quickly, refinancing to a shorter loan term, such as fifteen years instead of thirty, can save money on interest, though be warned—it will likely increase your monthly payments.

You can refinance any type of loan. Here's a list of loans you might have on a project, all of which can be refinanced:

- Conventional loans
- FHA (Federal Housing Administration) loans
- VA (Veteran's Assistance) loans
- USDA (United States Department of Agriculture) loans
- Hard money loans
- Private money loans
- Fix-and-flip loans
- Bridge loans
- Construction loans
- Owner-financed loans
- Asset-based loans
- Mezzanine loans
- Equity loans

Regardless of the loan type, refinancing can help you achieve your financial goals, whether it's lowering your interest rate, reducing monthly payments, or tapping into your property's equity.

So, what is refinancing? Refinancing means replacing your current mortgage with a new one, usually one with more favorable terms, like a lower interest rate. This process involves applying for a new loan that pays off your old one. The process typically includes comparing lenders, getting prequalified, submitting documents, going through underwriting, getting an appraisal, locking in your interest rate, and closing on the loan. Let's take a deeper look at each of those steps.

The Refinance Road Map

Step 1: Research and compare lenders
Research various lenders, including traditional banks, online lenders, credit unions, and mortgage brokers. Short-list lenders that offer competitive interest rates and terms, and then compare loan options from each of these lenders. Consider factors such as interest rates, fees (origination, closing, and appraisal), loan terms (repayment period, loan amount, and type), credit score requirements, and income and employment requirements. This will give you a comprehensive understanding of what each lender has to offer.

Step 2: Prequalification
Get an initial assessment of your eligibility based on factors like credit score and income. This report will help you understand potential loan options and which will be the best for you and your situation.

Step 3: Application and documentation
Complete a loan application and submit necessary documents, such as tax returns, pay stubs, and bank statements.

Step 4: Credit check and appraisal
The lender will check your credit report and order an appraisal to determine the current market value of your home.

Step 5: Underwriting
The lender will evaluate your financial profile—credit score, income, and home value—to decide whether to approve the loan and determine the terms.

Step 6: Loan estimate and lock-in

Review the loan estimate, which outlines the interest rate, fees, and loan terms. You can lock in the rate for a set period to protect against interest rate fluctuations.

Step 7: Closing day

Finalize the loan by signing the necessary documents and paying any closing costs to settle the new mortgage and pay off the old one.

Stage	Time Frame	Description
Preapproval	1–3 days	Initial application, credit check, and preapproval letter
Application and processing	7–14 days	Formal loan application, credit review, income and asset documentation
Underwriting	7–14 days	Loan package review, final decision, and potential requests for additional documentation
Appraisal and title review	3–7 days	Property value evaluation and title company review
Closing preparation	3–7 days	Closing document preparation and scheduling
Closing	1 day	Final loan document signing and ownership transfer

Overall Time Frame Estimates

Refinance Complexity	Time Frame
Straightforward refinance	30–60 days
Complex refinance or government-backed loan	60–90 days
Multiple properties, unique circumstances, or manual underwriting	90+ days

Typical Closing Costs

When refinancing a property, closing costs can vary depending on the lender, location, and type of loan. Here's a breakdown of estimated closing costs.

- Origination fee: 0.5–1% of the loan amount
- Discount points: 0.25–1% of the loan amount (optional)
- Appraisal fee: $300–$1,000
- Credit report fee: $30–$150
- Flood determination fee: $15–$50
- Title insurance and escrow fees: $1,500–$3,000
- Recording fees: $100–$500
- Mortgage broker fee: 0.5–2% of the loan amount (if applicable)
- Underwriting fee: $300–$900
- Survey fee: $500–$2,000 (if required)

Total Estimated Closing Costs
- 2–5 percent of the loan amount for conventional loans
- 1–3 percent of the loan amount for FHA loans
- 1–2 percent of the loan amount for VA loans

No-Closing-Cost Refinance Options
Some lenders offer no-closing-cost refinance options, which can save you money up front. However, these loans often come with higher interest rates or fees rolled into the loan, so be careful and thoroughly consider each option before committing one way or the other.

Tips to Minimize Closing Costs
- **Shop around:** Compare rates and fees from multiple lenders
- **Negotiate:** Ask your lender to waive or reduce certain fees
- **Consider a no-closing-cost refinance:** Weigh the pros and cons of this option
- **Look for lender credits:** Some lenders offer credits to offset closing costs

Remember to carefully review your loan estimate and closing disclosure to ensure you understand all the costs involved in your refinance.

I realize that a seven-step process is definitely a process, but hear me when I say the work is worth it. If market interest rates are lower than your current rate, refinancing can help you secure a lower interest rate and reduce your monthly payments. A general rule of thumb to follow is this: If you can get a rate at least 1 percent lower than your current one, refinance.

If your credit score has improved since taking out your original loan, refinancing could be a smart move. A better credit score can qualify you for a lower interest rate, saving you money on your monthly payments. This is especially true if you've made significant strides in improving your credit habits.

Perhaps you made some financial mistakes in the past, such as missing payments on a store credit card. However, if you've since turned things around by paying your bills on time and managing your debt responsibly, your credit score may have improved significantly. This newfound financial responsibility can be rewarded with a lower interest rate, leading to significant savings over the life of your loan.

Refinancing can also be a way to adjust your loan term—either shortening it to pay off your home sooner or lengthening it to reduce monthly payments. If you have an adjustable-rate mortgage (ARM) that is scheduled to reset soon, refinancing to a fixed-rate loan can lock in a stable rate and predictable payments. Additionally, refinancing allows you to tap into the equity in your home (provided you have at least 20 percent equity), which can help you eliminate private mortgage insurance (PMI) or access cash through a cash out refinance.

The best way to get started is to contact a lender to explore your refinancing options. You might be pleasantly surprised by the rates you qualify for.

The BRRRR Method

One very popular investing strategy that uses refinancing as a tool is the famous BRRRR strategy. BRRRR stands for buy, rehab, rent, refinance, and repeat.

- BUY a fixer-upper using short-term financing (e.g., private lender, joint venture (JV) partnership, hard money)
- REHAB/renovate the property to make it rent-ready
- RENT the units to begin generating income
- REFINANCE up to 70–75 percent of the after-repair value (ARV) to pay off the short-term financing
- REPEAT the process once your initial investment is returned through the refinance

I have used this strategy time and again to grow my portfolio in a very expensive West Coast market. The BRRRR method is good for all sizes of investments, big or small! (You can learn more about the BRRRR method in *Buy, Rehab, Rent, Refinance, Repeat* by David Green: www.BiggerPockets.com/ReadBRRRR.)

Case Study: A Real-Life Refinance Success Story to Inspire Your Next Move

Let me walk you through one of my favorite BRRRR deals. I once purchased a fourplex in Auburn, Washington, a growing suburb of Seattle with a solid rental market. The property features four townhome-style units, each offering 1,200 square feet of space with two bedrooms, two and a half bathrooms, a kitchen, living room, and both front and back decks. I acquired the property from an out-of-state investor who was looking to off-load it due to the challenges of managing it remotely. Here are the numbers:

- Purchase price: $625,000
- Total rehab: $185,000
- Financing: hard money

A hard money loan is a short-term, high-interest loan used for real estate investments, renovations, or business purposes. These loans are secured by collateral and often involve high fees and interest rates (10–18 percent). With flexible underwriting requirements, hard money loans can be used for fix-and-flip projects, rental property acquisitions, or for bridge debt options.

I financed 80 percent of acquisition at $500,000 and 100 percent of rehab at $185,000. I funded the remainder of the acquisition myself ($125,000 down payment).

I bought the property for $130 per square foot, significantly below the area's average of $240 per square foot.

The property was in pretty bad shape, and so I did a full-gut renovation.

Here is the scope of work completed:

- New roof
- New windows
- Updated kitchens, bathrooms, flooring, appliances
- New tile
- New exterior and interior paint
- All new flooring—laminate and carpet
- New decks and landscaping

I successfully transformed this property into a tenant haven, investing $31 per square foot in renovations. The result was four stunning units, each boasting modern, bright, and tenant-friendly features. The renovated property quickly attracted tenants, with each unit renting for $1,780 and generating a total monthly income of $7,120.

To capitalize on the property's increased value, I refinanced 70 percent of its ARV, which was appraised at $1.2 million (so I was able to cash out $840,000). This strategic move enabled me to pay off the short-term financing ($685,000—which included the purchase price and renovation budget) and recover my initial investment ($125,000—the down payment I paid out of pocket). As a bonus, I was able to get an additional $30,000 out of the refinance to keep this property ($840,000 - $685,000 - $125,000 = $30,000).

As evident in my situation, refinancing from a hard money loan to a long-term conventional loan proved to be a strategic decision. By doing so, I significantly reduced my interest rate from 11 to 3.75 percent. This move had a twofold benefit: It substantially increased my cash flow (by reducing the interest rate) and enabled me to execute a cash out refinance. The cash out refinance allowed me to pull out all the initial capital I had invested in the property, effectively recovering my entire investment.

Today, I proudly own a fourplex property with no money down, situated in an appreciating market and generating positive cash flow. With no initial investment remaining, my cash-on-cash return is infinite—a true testament to the power of strategic real estate investing.

I repeated the process, leveraging the property's equity to fuel further investments. I utilized the funds from the cash out refinance to acquire additional properties, including a duplex and another fourplex (remember, I was able to recoup my entire investment, pay off the hard money loan, pay myself back for the down payment, and make an extra $30,000!). I also renovated an office building, forcing appreciation and increasing its value.

In each case, I targeted undervalued assets, stabilized them through renovations and rental income, and then refinanced them to take advantage of cash out opportunities. This strategic approach has enabled me to continually grow my portfolio, leveraging the equity in each property to fuel further investments and drive long-term wealth creation.

Before we move forward, it's essential to highlight the versatility of refinancing. While many individuals use refinancing to consolidate debt or fund home improvements, others utilize the freed-up money for various purposes. Some people choose to stock an emergency fund, providing a financial safety net for unexpected expenses. Others may use the funds for educational purposes, such as covering a child's college tuition.

The beauty of refinancing lies in the flexibility it offers. Once you've freed up money through refinancing, you have the power to choose how you'll use it. Whether it's to achieve financial stability, invest in education, or simply enjoy some extra financial breathing room, refinancing can be a powerful tool in achieving your financial goals. Refinancing is a powerful tool, but it's just the beginning. The real magic happens when you combine refinancing with a clear vision, a solid strategy, and a commitment to taking action.

So, what does this mean for you? Here are five key takeaways, one for each character. Pick the one that works best for you and your own real estate adventure.

NEW-TO-THE-GAME NOAH

As a newcomer to refinancing, it's essential to start with the basics. Focus on understanding how refinancing can impact your financial situation, particularly in terms of lowering your monthly payments or building an emergency fund.

Key Benefits for Beginners:
- Lower monthly payments: Refinancing can help reduce your monthly expenses, freeing up more money for savings, investments, or unexpected costs
- Building an emergency fund: By refinancing, you can tap into your home's equity and create a financial safety net for future expenses or unexpected events

Finding Guidance and Support

As a beginner, it's invaluable to have a mentor or guide to help you navigate the refinancing process. Consider the following options:

- Personal network: Reach out to friends, family, or colleagues who have experience with refinancing
- Bank or lender: Visit a bank or consult with a lender who can provide personalized guidance and support

Remember, refinancing can be a powerful tool for managing your finances. Take your time, do your research, and don't hesitate to seek help when needed. These can feel like big steps and a lot to take on, but I know you! You've got that underdog, new-to-the-game energy and you can do this!

ACTIVE ALEX

As an active investor, you're poised to take your portfolio to the next level. By implementing forced appreciation strategies, you'll be able to add significant value to your properties. This could include renovations, repositioning, or rebranding to increase rental income or attract higher-paying tenants.

The Power of Refinancing

Once you've forced appreciation, the next step is to refinance your properties to access the increased equity. This will provide you with the funds needed to:

- Tackle new projects or renovations.
- Expand your portfolio through strategic acquisitions.
- Diversify your investments and reduce risk.

Scaling Your Portfolio

As an active investor, you thrive on reinvesting and growing your portfolio. By unlocking cash through refinancing, you'll be able to:

- Accelerate your investment strategy.
- Pursue new opportunities and partnerships.
- Build a more robust and resilient portfolio.

This is an exciting opportunity for you to scale your investments and achieve your goals. By combining forced appreciation and refinancing, you'll be unstoppable!

PIVOT PEYTON

As you navigate the ever-changing real estate landscape, refinancing can be a powerful tool to provide the flexibility you need. By refinancing properties with significant equity, you can generate cash to fuel new ventures and pivot into fresh opportunities.

Exploring New Avenues

Refinancing can provide the necessary funds to:

- Make a down payment on a different type of property, such as an apartment building or commercial space.
- Expand into a new market, capitalizing on emerging trends and opportunities.
- Transition into a new real estate niche, such as fix-and-flip projects or rental properties.

Seizing New Opportunities

By refinancing and pivoting your strategy, you can:

- Diversify your portfolio and reduce risk.
- Increase your potential for returns and growth.
- Stay adaptable and responsive to changing market conditions.

Refinancing can be the catalyst for your next move. Consider how you can leverage your existing properties to fuel your next venture and take your real estate investments to the next level.

SEASONED-INVESTOR SAM

As a seasoned investor, you're well positioned to leverage refinancing as a powerful tool for portfolio optimization. By identifying properties with significant equity or high interest rates, you can refinance to:

- Increase cash flow and enhance profitability.
- Consolidate debt and simplify your financial landscape.
- Free up capital for larger projects, long-term investments, and strategic initiatives.

Maximizing Impact

With a diversified portfolio, you have numerous opportunities to refinance and make a significant impact on your bottom line. By refinancing multiple properties, you can:

- Amplify cash flow increases and debt consolidation benefits.
- Unlock substantial capital for strategic investments and growth initiatives.
- Enhance your overall financial standing and portfolio resilience.

Refinancing is a strategic move that can help you optimize your portfolio, increase profitability, and achieve your long-term investment goals.

LONG-GAME LOGAN

As a patient investor, you're poised to leverage refinancing as a strategic tool for long-term growth. By waiting for market appreciation to build equity naturally, you can:

- Refinance to access funds for wealth-building opportunities.
- Invest in additional properties or other long-term ventures.
- Gradually grow your portfolio and increase your net worth.

Aligning with Your Long-Term Vision

This refinancing strategy perfectly complements your commitment to gradual growth over time. By focusing on long-term appreciation and strategic refinancing, you can:

- Avoid get-rich-quick schemes and focus on sustainable growth.
- Build a resilient portfolio that withstands market fluctuations.
- Achieve long-term financial success and security.

Stick to your strategy—compound growth is on your side, Long-Game Logan! Your patience and strategic approach will pay off in the long run.

Chapter 8

The ADU Advantage—Boosting Your Bottom Line

An "income-producing unit" in real estate is a property (or part of a property) that earns its own income. Think of an income-producing unit like a mini business inside your larger investment property. Some income-producing units that can add value to a property include commercial spaces, storage units, vacation rentals, and my favorite: accessory dwelling units (ADUs) and detached accessory dwelling units (DADUs).

Income-producing units in real estate come in many forms, and their value is undeniable. They can significantly boost a property's overall worth in a few key ways.

- They generate a steady and predictable stream of income—typically through rent or other income-producing features. This additional cash flow not only enhances your current returns but also makes the property more appealing to future buyers and investors.
- Income-producing units can appreciate in value over time, providing a potential long-term capital gain. This combination of income generation and appreciation can lead to attractive total returns.
- Income-generating properties may qualify for better financing terms, such as lower interest rates or larger loan amounts, and specialized financing options, such as commercial mortgages or apartment building loans, making them easy to set up and leverage.
- Having multiple income-producing units can provide a diversified income stream, reducing dependence on a single source of income. This can be especially beneficial in times of economic uncertainty.

- A property with strong income potential is often easier to sell and can command a higher price, making it a win-win for any investor.

Another great aspect of this type of investment is the wide variety in which you can apply it. By incorporating these units into a property, owners and investors can unlock significant value and the potential for long-term returns.

Let's dive into my favorite types of income-producing units, ADUs and DADUs. Both ADUs and DADUs are secondary residential units built on a property that already has a primary dwelling.

Key Characteristics

The abbreviations ADUs and DADUs are often used interchangeably, but there can be subtle differences depending on local regulations and zoning laws.

- **ADUs:** Can be attached or detached from the main house, offering flexibility in design and placement
- **DADUs:** Are stand-alone structures, providing a separate and independent living space

And in case that wasn't confusing enough, a detached ADU is not always the same as a DADU. In general, both detached ADUs and DADUs refer to separate, freestanding structures that provide additional living space. However, some jurisdictions might distinguish between the two terms based on factors like:

- **Size:** DADUs might be limited to a specific size, while detached ADUs could be larger
- **Location:** DADUs might be restricted to certain areas of the property, while detached ADUs could be placed elsewhere
- **Amenities:** DADUs might require separate utilities, while detached ADUs could share utilities with the primary dwelling

In many cases, though, the terms "detached ADU" and "DADU" are used synonymously to describe a separate, freestanding residential unit on a property.

The Rise of the ADU Empire

ADUs and DADUs are game changers in urban areas. Not only do they offer a more affordable housing option for both homeowners and renters but they're also much easier to build because of their reduced permitting timelines and reduced need for new development. They also utilize a piece of an investor's existing land holdings, speeding up the process.

Plus, they're crazy flexible—think in-law suites, tiny homes, a guest house, a casita, or separate units. As the demand for ADUs/DADUs continues to soar, it's clear that these tiny but mighty units are here to stay—and revolutionize the housing market in the process. And bonus, because of their flexibility, this strategy is one anyone can tap into, whether you are a New-to-the-Game Noah or Long-Game Logan!

How to Identify the Perfect Property

All of my good stories start with me buying a house to flip. In 2017, I bought a single-family house that I planned to renovate and sell. *A quick six-month flip!* I told myself. As I started working on the house, I realized that the basement would make a perfect mother-in-law suite—a type of ADU. It had its own entrance, a nice wet bar, a bedroom, and a bathroom. After working with my architect, I was able to convert the wet bar into a kitchen, add a second bedroom, and even create a living space. This unit would now easily rent for $3,500/month. I had just unlocked the potential of income-generating units.

My projected ARV for this house was $970,000, but by adding the income-generating unit, my buyers were able to afford a higher mortgage payment, and we ended up with multiple offers, ultimately selling the house for $1,150,000—a dramatic increase of $180,000 additional profit.

Truly, the possibilities for this strategy are endless, but I'm a big fan of learning through examples, so let me show you a few ways to make this magic happen.

Here are some popular types of ADUs to consider.

- **Garage conversions:** Converting an existing garage into a living space

- **Basement conversions:** Converting an existing basement into a living space
- **Attic conversions:** Converting an existing attic into a living space
- **Accessory structures and backyard cottages:** Building a separate structure, such as a guest house or in-law suite

Before you get started, I want you to know one important thing: It is essential to research local zoning laws and regulations regarding ADUs. It is imperative that you ensure the property is zoned for ADUs and that it complies with local ordinances.

Next, look for properties with sufficient space for an ADU, such as a large backyard or an underutilized garage. Another possibility is to consider properties with existing structures that can be converted.

Neighborhood demand is also crucial. Research the local rental market and demand for housing, identifying neighborhoods with high demand for affordable housing options. Next, calculate the potential revenue from renting out the ADU and consider construction costs, financing, and ongoing expenses to ensure financial feasibility.

Finally, think about the design and layout of the ADU, including its size, location, and amenities, ensuring along the way that it meets local building codes and regulations.

So, what do you think? Are you ready to take the ADU plunge? While converting an existing space is often the easier route, building a DADU can be highly beneficial for your investment property. If you're feeling adventurous and ready to dive in, I've got you covered! The rest of this chapter lays out my comprehensive guide to helping you navigate the process, from finding the perfect lot to securing financing and bringing your detached ADU vision to life.

Identify the Perfect Lot

Every city has its own zoning and regulations when it comes to ADUs and DADUs. It is important to not only get the lowdown on the rules and regulations in your area but to move forward in compliance.

Here are the initial questions I would recommend that you ask.

- What is the minimum size requirement for an ADU?
- What are the setback regulations?

Setback regulations require buildings to be constructed a minimum distance from property lines, streets, and neighboring structures. These rules vary by location and are governed by zoning laws, municipal codes, and neighborhood covenants. Setbacks help maintain property boundaries, preserve public spaces, and protect environmental areas.

- Do any of the units need to be owner occupied?
- Can the units be used as rentals?
- Is it possible to sell an ADU separately from the primary residence?

In Seattle, the size of a DADU must not exceed a total of 1,000 square feet of occupiable space, while the minimum lot size required is 3,200 square feet. For an attached accessory dwelling unit (AADU), regulations stipulate that it is subject to the size of the primary unit.

To find your city's DADU laws, start by visiting your city's official website planning and zoning websites. Look for sections on zoning regulations, land use, or building codes. Some cities also have dedicated pages for DADUs or ADUs.

You can also try:

- **Municipal codes:** Search for your city's municipal code online, which often outlines zoning regulations and DADU laws
- **City planning department:** Contact your city's planning department directly to ask about DADU laws and regulations
- **Local government website:** Check your local government website for information on building codes, zoning laws, and DADU regulations

To determine if a property is suitable for a DADU, it's essential to utilize online resources. In Seattle, there's a dedicated website called ADUniverse, which allows you to type in any Seattle address and find out if a DADU can be placed on the property. Look for similar resources in your city that provide DADU information and zoning regulations

Another good approach is to connect with land-use planners in your city's construction and permitting department. These experts have access to a wealth of information, including property characteristics and current zoning laws, which can help you determine if a property is suitable for your DADU project.

Purchasing a distressed SFH on a spacious lot, ripe for a DADU addition, is a savvy investment strategy. This approach can unlock a treasure trove of passive income through rental opportunities or property sales. In cities like Seattle, DADUs can be split and sold off separately to two different buyers, or you can sell one and hold the other as a rental. This flexibility offers multiple exit strategies that cater to various investor goals and priorities, making it a versatile strategy for anyone.

Finding the Ideal Spot for Your DADU

When searching for the perfect lot to build a DADU, consider the following types:

- **Dual-frontage lots:** The holy grail of lots! Rare and valuable, these lots offer two street frontages, providing unique development opportunities.
- **Corner lots:** Located at street intersections, corner lots often provide more space and flexibility for DADU design
- **Large rectangular lots:** Long, narrow lots offer ample space for a DADU, with room for parking and outdoor areas
- **Flag lots:** Lots with narrow entrances leading to wider, private areas are perfect for DADUs
- **Subdividable lots:** Larger lots that can be subdivided into smaller parcels allow for the creation of a new lot for the DADU (more on this in the next chapter!)
- **Underutilized lots:** Lots with existing homes that have underutilized space, such as large backyards or unused garages, are ideal for converting into a DADU
- **Vacant lots:** Empty lots offer a blank slate for building a DADU from scratch
- **Lots with alley access:** Lots with alley access provide a convenient location for a DADU, often with fewer zoning restrictions

Dual-frontage lots

Corner lots

Large rectangular lots

Flag lots

Subdividable lots

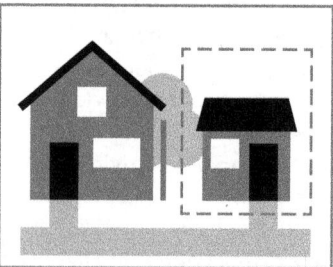

Underutilized lots

Vacant lots

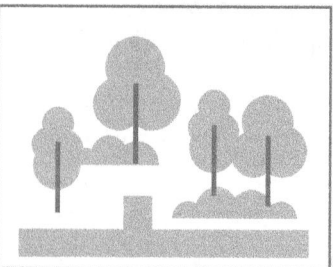

Lots with alley access

Funding Your ADU or DADU

Financing an ADU or DADU project involves multiple steps, requiring lenders who can navigate each phase. Here's a breakdown of the process.

1. **Acquiring the SFH:** Initial purchase of the property
2. **Renovating the SFH:** Financing for renovations and upgrades
3. **Permitting and building the DADU:** Funding for construction and necessary permits
4. **Splitting the units:** Survey and land-use attorney fees to establish an HOA and separate the units

Understanding Partial Lien Releases and Types of Liens

To facilitate selling one unit and keeping the other, lenders must permit a partial lien release. A partial lien release is a legal document that releases a portion of a property from a lien while leaving the remaining portion of the property still encumbered by the lien. The remaining loan is then paid off when the retained property is refinanced into a long-term loan.

A "lien" is a legal claim placed on a property (or another type of asset, such as a vehicle or jewelry) to ensure that a debt is repaid. Essentially, it acts as a hold, giving the creditor the right to seize and sell the property if the borrower fails to pay. Creditors, such as banks, contractors, or even the government, use liens to secure debts and guarantee payment. If a borrower falls behind on payments, the creditor can file a lien, and if the debt remains unpaid, they may ultimately foreclose on the property to recover what they are owed. There are several types of liens, each serving a different purpose.

Types of Liens
- **Mortgage lien:** A lien against a property secured by a mortgage.
- **Tax lien:** A lien placed on property for unpaid taxes.
- **Judgment lien:** A lien placed on property after a court judgment for a debt
- **Mechanic's lien:** A lien placed on property for unpaid work or materials on a property

In the context of lot subdivisions, a partial lien release is often used when a lender has a lien on the entire subdivision property, but the borrower wants to sell off individual lots. The partial lien release allows the lender to release their lien on the specific lot being sold while maintaining their lien on the remaining lots.

This process enables the borrower to:

- Sell individual lots without having to pay off the entire loan.
- Use the proceeds from the lot sale to pay down the loan or fund further development.
- Continue to develop and sell the remaining lots while still having access to financing.

Partial lien releases typically require:

- Approval from the lender.
- A review of the property's survey and plat map to ensure the release is accurate.
- Recording of the partial lien release with the local county records office.

By using partial lien releases, borrowers can manage their cash flow, reduce their debt burden, and continue to develop and sell their subdivision property.

In my experience, not all lenders do partial lien releases. Sometimes, if the lender has not previously agreed to it, they can "call the note," which means you would have to pay off the lender the whole amount if you own a portion of the property that the lender has a deed on. It is extremely important to clearly communicate your plans and subdivision intentions with your lender beforehand.

There are several types of lenders you can work with to finance your ADU or DADU, including:

- **Construction lenders:** Specialized lenders that provide financing for land development, including lot subdivisions
- **Private money lenders:** Nontraditional lenders that offer short-term, high-interest loans for real estate development projects

- **Hard-money lenders:** Similar to private money lenders, hard-money lenders provide short-term, asset-based loans for real estate investments
- **Community banks:** Local banks that may offer construction financing and partial lien releases for lot subdivisions
- **Regional banks:** Larger banks with a regional presence that may offer construction financing and partial lien releases
- **Specialty lenders:** Lenders that focus on specific types of real estate projects, such as land development or lot subdivisions
- **Mezzanine lenders:** Lenders that provide subordinate financing for real estate projects, which can be used in conjunction with senior construction loans

Navigating the Permitting and Building Process for DADUs

The permitting process for DADUs is notably simpler and faster compared to new construction homes.

To apply for permits for ADUs in your city, you'll typically need to visit your local government's planning or building department. Here are some steps to follow.

- **Check your city's website:** Look for information on ADU permits, applications, and requirements on your city's official website
- **Visit the planning department:** Reach out to your local planning department to inquire about the application process, required documents, and fees
- **Submit your application:** Fill out the application form, usually available online or in person, and submit it along with the required documents, such as property deeds, site plans, and architectural drawings
- **Architects:** Consult a local architect, as they have extensive knowledge of local building codes, zoning regulations, and permitting processes, making it easier for them to navigate the complexities of different cities' codes

Some cities also offer online portals or webforms to initiate the application process, so look for your city's Department of Construction and Inspections portal.

The key advantages of this approach are numerous. With fewer inspections, regulatory hurdles are significantly reduced, streamlining the process. Additionally, relaxed zoning regulations offer more flexibility in design and placement, providing greater creative freedom. Furthermore, the faster plan review process expedites approval, allowing projects to move forward more quickly and efficiently.

Timeline Comparison

- **New construction home:** Twelve to fourteen months for permit approval
- **DADU:** Six to eight weeks for permit approval

Additional Benefits

- **Lower permit fees:** Cost savings for developers
- **Reduced timelines:** Faster project completion, typically within eight months

Overall, the streamlined permitting and building process for DADUs makes them an attractive option for developers and property owners.

To provide clarity on the DADU construction process, I've outlined the steps involved. Understanding these phases is crucial, as it offers a comprehensive overview of what to expect during the project.

Phase 1: Preconstruction Phase

1. **Prework:** Initial planning and preparation
2. **Architect/engineering:** Design and engineering services
3. **Prework demo:** Demolition and removal of existing structures (if necessary)
4. **Site prep:** Preparation of the building site
5. **Permit fees for application:** Submission of permit applications and payment of associated fees

Phase 2: Construction Phase

With permits in hand, the building process begins.

1. **Permit issued:** Receive official approval to start construction
2. **Break ground:** Commence excavation and site work
3. **Trench work:** Dig trenches for utility lines and other underground infrastructure
4. **Drainage:** Install drainage systems to manage water flow
5. **Foundation:** Lay the foundation for the DADU, including footings and slab
6. **Concrete:** Pour concrete for the foundation, slab, and other structural elements
7. **Framing:** Construct the frame of the DADU, including walls and roof
8. **Roof:** Install roofing materials, such as shingles or tiles
9. **Sheathing:** Add exterior sheathing to the frame, preparing it for exterior finishes

Phase 3: Interior Progress

The building process continues with.

1. **Rough-ins completed:** Installation of plumbing, HVAC, and electrical systems is finished
2. **Drywall started:** Hanging and finishing of drywall begins to create smooth walls and ceilings
3. **Cabinets and ordering completed:** All cabinets, fixtures, and materials needed for the trim-out phase have been ordered and are ready for installation

Phase 4: Final Inspection

1. All utilities connected
2. Final inspection clearance
3. Certificate of occupancy issued

When and How to Create a Homeowners Association for Your DADU

In King County (Greater Seattle Area), creating a homeowners association (HOA) for a DADU is required if the lot is being subdivided and the DADU is being sold separately. This requirement applies to both land subdivisions and DADU additions. However, if the lot is not being subdivided and the DADU is not being sold separately, an HOA may not be necessary. It's essential to consult with local authorities and/or an attorney to determine the specific requirements for your project.

When an HOA Is Typically Required
- **Two separate units:** When a DADU is built on a property with an existing SFH, and the two units will be owned separately, an HOA may be required to manage shared responsibilities and resolve potential disputes
- **Shared common areas:** If the DADU and the primary residence share common areas, such as a driveway, yard, or utilities, an HOA can help manage these shared spaces
- **Local regulations:** Some municipalities may require the creation of an HOA for DADUs, especially if the units are intended for rental or sale

Benefits of Creating an HOA for DADUs
- **Clarifies responsibilities:** An HOA can establish clear guidelines for maintenance, repairs, and decision-making processes
- **Manages shared expenses:** An HOA can help manage shared expenses, such as utility costs, insurance, and maintenance
- **Resolves disputes:** An HOA can provide a framework for resolving disputes between owners, helping maintain a positive living environment

Alternatives to Creating an HOA
- **Joint ownership agreement:** Owners can enter into a joint ownership agreement, outlining shared responsibilities and decision-making processes
- **Shared maintenance agreement:** Owners can create a shared maintenance agreement, specifying how shared expenses and maintenance tasks will be handled

Ultimately, whether to create an HOA for a DADU depends on the city's jurisdictions. It's essential to consult with your city planning department and carefully consider the options before making a decision.

Finding Your Dream Builder

Now that you have a clear understanding of the project, it's time to find the perfect builder to bring your vision to life. Selecting the right builder is crucial, as it will not only impact the quality of the final project but also affect your daily life and stress levels throughout the process. Investing time in finding a reliable and skilled builder is essential.

Here are some effective ways to find a trustworthy builder for your DADU project.

- **Word of mouth:** Ask friends, family, or neighbors who have completed similar projects for recommendations
- **Online reviews:** Check websites like Yelp, Google, or Angie's List for reviews and ratings of local builders
- **Professional associations:** Contact local builders' associations, such as the National Association of Home Builders (NAHB), for a list of reputable builders in your area
- **Social media:** Utilize social media platforms like Facebook or LinkedIn to ask for recommendations or search for local builders
- **Local listings:** Check online directories like Houzz or Thumbtack for builders in your area
- **Better Business Bureau (BBB):** Verify a builder's reputation and check for any complaints filed with the BBB
- **Get multiple bids:** Invite several builders to bid on your project to compare prices, services, and qualifications
- **Check licenses and certifications:** Verify a builder's licenses, certifications, and insurance coverage to ensure they meet local requirements
- **Portfolio and references:** Review a builder's portfolio and ask for references to assess their experience and work quality
- **Interview potential builders:** Conduct in-person interviews to discuss your project, their approach, and your expectations

Additionally, I suggest you ask the experts who work behind the scenes. I've had the best luck finding top-tier teams by asking my trusted subcontractors—electricians, plumbers, HVAC specialists—which builders and general contractors they enjoy working with. Their referrals have consistently paid off because they can personally vouch for the people who demonstrate a strong work ethic, reliability, and fair business practices. This includes showing up on time, paying subcontractors promptly and fairly, and maintaining a positive and professional work environment.

Calculating the ROI of Your ADU Investment

Determining the ROI of your ADU is crucial to understanding its financial viability. I hate to sound like a broken record, but truly, no matter how much you enjoy the process, your goal is to make money. If the numbers don't make sense, you are working yourself into a hard hole to climb out of.

Here's a step-by-step guide to help you calculate the ROI of your ADU.

Step 1: Determine your ADU's income potential
- **(Long-term) rent:** Research the local rental market to determine a fair monthly rent for your ADU
- **(Short-term) Airbnb:** If you plan to rent your ADU on Airbnb, estimate the average nightly rate and occupancy rate

Step 2: Calculate your ADU's annual income
- **(Long-term) monthly rent:** Multiply the monthly rent by twelve to get the annual rent
- **(Short-term) Airbnb income:** Multiply the average nightly rate by the number of nights you hope to book per year

Step 3: Calculate your ADU's expenses
- **Mortgage payments:** If you financed your ADU, calculate your monthly mortgage payments and multiply by twelve
- **Property taxes:** Estimate your annual property taxes on the ADU
- **Insurance:** Calculate your annual insurance premiums for the ADU

- **Maintenance and repairs:** Estimate your annual maintenance and repair costs
- **Utilities:** If you're responsible for paying utilities, estimate your annual costs

If you find yourself needing more guidance on the intricacies of these calculations, check out the book *Real Estate by the Numbers* from J Scott and Dave Meyer. It's a great reference tool and book to have in your personal finance library, and you can get from on the BiggerPockets bookstore: www.BiggerPockets.com/ReadByTheNumbers.

Step 4: Calculate your ADU's net operating income (NOI)
- Subtract your ADU's expenses from its annual income to get the NOI

Step 5: Calculate your ADU's ROI
- Divide the NOI by the total cost of building the ADU (including construction costs, permits, and inspections)
- Multiply the result by one hundred to express the ROI as a percentage

If you're like me and learn best by seeing the strategy in action, let's look at an example. Let's say you added a mother-in-law suite to your property.

Annual income:
$30,000 (long-term rental) or $40,000 (Airbnb, STR)

Expenses:
$10,000 (mortgage payments) + $2,000 (property taxes) + $1,500 (insurance) + $1,000 (maintenance and repairs) + $1,000 (utilities) = $16,500

NOI:
$30,000 (long-term rental) - $16,500 (expenses) = $13,500 or $40,000 (Airbnb, STR) - $16,500 (expenses) = $23,500

ROI:
($13,500 ÷ $150,000) x 100 = 9% (long-term rent rental) or ($23,500 ÷ $150,000) x 100 = 15.67% (Airbnb, STR)

Category	Long-Term Rent	Airbnb
Annual income	$30,000	$40,000
Expenses	$16,500	$16,500
Mortgage payments	$10,000	$10,000
Property taxes	$2,000	$2,000
Insurance	$1,500	$1,500
Maintenance & repairs	$1,000	$1,000
Utilities	$1,000	$1,000
NOI	$13,500	$23,500
ROI	9%	15.67%
Investment amount	$150,000	$150,000

By following these steps, you'll be able to calculate the ROI of your ADU and make informed decisions about your investment.

Case Study: Transforming a Distressed Property into a DADU Opportunity

In 2023, I purchased a distressed SFH in Seattle. I immediately recognized the potential of its through lot to accommodate a DADU, thus unlocking a valuable investment opportunity.

Property background
- Location: Seattle, Washington
- Property type: Single-family home
- Purchase price: $560,000 (distressed sale)
- Property condition: Needed a full-gut renovation
- Property was 890 square feet, with two bedrooms and two bathrooms
- Lot size: 5,000 square feet
- Zoning: Allows for a DADU

Goals for the project

- Buy a distressed property in Seattle
- Renovate the main house
- Build a DADU in the backyard for long-term rent
- Generate passive income through rental properties

Property renovation

- Main house renovation:
  - Budget: $125,000
  - Scope: New siding, electrical, plumbing, landscaping, flooring, paint, kitchen and bathroom renovations
  - Timeline: Eight months
- DADU Construction:
  - Budget: $400,000
  - Scope: 1,000-square-foot, two-bedroom, 2.5-bathroom DADU with a small yard
  - Timeline: Eight months

Financing

- Purchase price: $560,000
- Down payment: 15% ($84,000)
- Hard money loan: $476,000 at 9% interest
- Renovation loan: $100,000 at 9% interest
- DADU construction loan: $385,000 at 9% interest

Exit values

- Main house sale: $675,000
- DADU appraised value: $725,000

Achieving a Successful Project Outcome

Our project's total expense of $1,045,000 yielded a remarkable exit value of $1,400,000, demonstrating a substantial ROI. By strategically selling the main house and refinancing the DADU, we eliminated all debt, enabling us to retain the DADU with zero out-of-pocket expenses.

Plus, the DADU allowed a great opportunity to hold as a long-term rental.

Expenses

- Mortgage payments: $2,700/month
- Property taxes: $110/month

- Insurance: $50/month
- Maintenance and repairs: $50/month
- Property management: $240/month
- Total expenses: $3,350/month

Cash Flow

- Monthly cash flow: $250 ($3,400 rental income - $3,150 expenses)
- Annual cash flow: $3,000

While the annual cash flow may not be spectacular, the potential for long-term appreciation in property value and rental income makes this investment worth considering. In an expensive market like Seattle, it is rare to cash flow and appreciate with no money out of pocket! And remember, every little bit adds up. The more of these you build, the more your bottom line will grow.

The picture above is a DADU plus a single-family home. The following pictures are the DADU and single-family home photographed separately

This was a long chapter—well done for making it to the end! There's a lot to absorb, so let's simplify things. Below is a clear, strategic takeaway for each character profile—something you can hold onto and apply as you move forward.

If you don't yet own a property, this is your moment to buy smart. Look for homes on large lots, on corner parcels, or with existing garages or basements that can be converted into ADUs. Focus on areas with favorable zoning and rental demand. Starting with a property that has ADU or DADU potential sets you up for future cash flow, equity growth, and exit flexibility—all while learning the ropes of real estate investing from a strong foundation.

Why ADUs and DADUs?

- Low-risk entry point: ADUs and DADUs offer a relatively low-risk way to enter the real estate investing market
- Leverage existing spaces: You can start by converting existing spaces, such as basements or garages, into income-producing units
- Build experience: As you gain experience, you can expand your investments and explore new opportunities

Key Takeaways

- Start small: Begin with a single unit or a small project to gain experience and build your confidence
- Focus on learning: Educate yourself on the basics of ADUs and DADUs, including local regulations, financing options, and property management
- Be patient: Real estate investing is a long-term game. Be prepared to put in the time and effort required to succeed.

Just Start!

Don't be afraid to take the first step. With dedication and hard work, you can build a successful real estate investing business. Remember, the key is to start small, learn as you go, and continually work toward your goals.

🔨 ACTIVE ALEX

To boost your cash flow, focus on identifying underutilized spaces in your current portfolio that can be converted into ADUs. Here's a strategic approach.

Prioritize Properties and Markets

- High-demand rentals: Focus on properties in areas with high demand for rentals, ensuring a steady stream of income
- Urban or infill locations: Target urban or infill locations with limited housing supply, increasing the potential for rental income

Ensure Compliance

- Local zoning laws: Verify compliance with local zoning laws and regulations to avoid costly delays or fines
- Streamline the process: Ensure you have all necessary permits and approvals before commencing construction

Key Benefits

- Increased cash flow: ADUs can provide a significant boost to your rental income
- Improved property value: Adding ADUs can increase your property's value and appeal to potential buyers
- Diversified income streams: ADUs can provide a secondary income stream, reducing reliance on a single rental property

By prioritizing high-demand markets and ensuring compliance with local regulations, you can maximize your portfolio's potential and enjoy increased cash flow and property value.

PIVOT PEYTON

Consider leveraging ADUs to adapt to changing market conditions and diversify your income streams. Here are two pivot strategies.

- Subdivide lots: Divide your property into separate parcels, allowing you to sell or rent individual units
- Sell one unit, retain another: Sell one unit to realize a profit, while keeping another unit for ongoing rental income

Before You Pivot

- Crunch the numbers: Analyze the financial implications of each option

- Align with evolving goals: Ensure your pivot strategy aligns with your changing investment objectives

By pivoting your investment approach with ADUs, you can:

- Diversify your income streams.
- Adapt to changing market demands.
- Achieve your evolving investment goals.

Take the first step, crunch the numbers, and pivot your investment strategy to stay ahead in the game!

💼 SEASONED-INVESTOR SAM

As a seasoned investor, you can leverage your expertise and network to efficiently execute ADU projects. Here's a strategic approach.

Efficient Project Execution
- Delegate tasks: Focus on high-level decision-making and delegate tasks to experts, such as contractors, architects, and financiers
- Leverage your network: Utilize your professional network to access top talent, financing options, and valuable insights

Strategic Lot Selection
- Target dual-frontage or corner lots: These lots offer maximum value and flexibility, allowing for multiple exit strategies
- Unlock multiple income streams: Dual-frontage or corner lots can accommodate multiple ADUs, increasing potential rental income

Key Benefits
- Maximized returns: Strategic lot selection and efficient project execution can lead to higher returns on investment
- Reduced risk: Delegating tasks and leveraging your network can minimize risks associated with ADU projects
- Increased flexibility: Multiple exit strategies provide flexibility in responding to changing market conditions

⏱ LONG-GAME LOGAN

To create a foundation for long-term wealth creation, consider adopting ADUs as a core strategy. Here's a forward-thinking approach.

Focus on Scalability and Sustainability

- Scalable projects: Develop ADUs that can be easily replicated, allowing for efficient expansion and increased returns
- Sustainable designs: Incorporate eco-friendly features and materials to reduce environmental impact and attract environmentally conscious tenants

Align with Future Housing Trends

- Affordability: Focus on creating affordable housing options to address the growing demand for budget-friendly rentals
- Urban density: Prioritize properties in urban areas with high population density, ensuring a steady demand for housing

Key Benefits

- Long-term relevance: By aligning with future housing trends, your ADU investments will remain relevant for decades to come
- Increased demand: Focus on affordability and urban density to capitalize on the growing demand for housing in these areas
- Wealth creation: Scalable and sustainable ADU projects can generate significant long-term wealth through rental income and property appreciation

By adopting ADUs as a cornerstone of your long-term wealth creation strategy, you can build a sustainable and profitable portfolio that will thrive for generations.

Chapter 9

Subdivision Success—Carving Out New Opportunities

It was a typical day in 2017 when I closed the deal on a house that would change everything. The property was a split-entry, 2,400-square-foot home, nestled on a sprawling lot of almost an acre. As I walked through the doors, I couldn't shake the feeling that there was more to this property than met the eye. I decided to take a drive around the neighborhood, curious about the surrounding homes. That's when I saw it: a large land-use sign indicating that a nearby lot was being subdivided.

The thought hit me: *What if I could do the same with my own lot?* This idea had never occurred to me before, but I suddenly couldn't stop thinking about it. I quickly assessed my new property, noting that it was flatter and bigger than my neighbor's. The wheels began to turn, and I knew somehow that it would work—and that I had to try it.

What came next was a four-year odyssey. The subdivision process was grueling, requiring endless permits, paperwork, and perseverance. There were times when it seemed like the odds were stacked against me, but I refused to give up.

And then, finally, after years of blood, sweat, and tears, I succeeded in dividing my lot into three separate parcels, with the original house sitting proudly on one of them and the other two open for new possibilities. Not only that, but in making this amazing project happen, I had achieved something else just as remarkable—my very first seven-figure profit.

What Are Lot Subdivisions?

Lot subdivisions aren't as widely talked about as most of the other investment opportunities in this book. If I hadn't seen my neighbors take up this opportunity, I wouldn't have even known it existed. And I'll be clear up front—making subdivisions happen is no walk in the park. But if you're willing to learn how they work and have some patience and perseverance, they can be a uniquely lucrative way to diversify your portfolio.

Lot subdivision is the process of dividing a single parcel of land into two or more smaller parcels, each with its own separate ownership and boundaries. Each parcel can now be developed, built on, rented out, and/or sold independently of the others. This process involves working with local government agencies to obtain the necessary approvals and permits to subdivide the land.

Lot subdivisions can be used for various purposes, such as:

- **Developing new homes:** Subdividing a large parcel of land can create multiple building lots for new homes
- **Creating commercial properties:** Subdividing land can also create separate parcels for commercial development, such as office buildings, retail spaces, or restaurants
- **Investment opportunities:** Lot subdivisions can provide investors with opportunities to buy, subdivide, and sell land for a profit
- **Estate planning:** Subdividing land can also be used as an estate planning tool, allowing property owners to divide their land among family members or heirs

All of these purposes can increase returns and/or provide additional opportunities for investors like you and me! Let's dive into the subdivision process.

Understanding Zoning, Permits, and Other Challenges

Subdividing land can be a complex and daunting process, especially when it comes to navigating the intricacies of zoning, permits, and regulations. To ensure a successful subdivision project, it's essential to have a solid understanding of these critical components.

First, research local zoning codes to determine what properties in your area are eligible for subdivision. This involves:

- **Minimum lot sizes:** Verifying the minimum lot size requirements to ensure that subdivided parcels will meet the necessary standards

- **Setback requirements:** Understanding the required setbacks from property lines, roads, and other features to ensure compliance
- **Density restrictions:** Familiarizing yourself with density restrictions, such as the maximum number of units allowed per acre

Note: You can find links to your local zoning laws and regulations websites from www.BiggerPockets.com/ROIBookBonus.

Once you have a clear understanding of these codes, you can easily determine whether a property is a candidate for subdivision or not.

Next, you need to understand securing subdivision permits. This involves several steps, including:

- **Environmental impact assessments:** Conducting assessments to identify potential environmental impacts, such as wetlands, endangered species, or water quality concerns. Environmentally critical areas (ECAs) can be the death of lot developments.
- **Traffic impact assessments:** Evaluating the potential impact of the subdivision on local traffic patterns and infrastructure
- **Subdivision permit application:** Submitting a comprehensive permit application, including detailed plans, specifications, and supporting documentation
- **Timelines and costs:** Understanding the timelines and costs associated with subdivision approvals, including permit fees, inspection costs, and potential delays
- **Trees:** My city has a lot of rules and regulations when it comes to cutting down trees. We had to plant fourteen new plants for every tree that was cut down. Partner with an arborist!

Finally, subdivision projects often encounter challenges that require careful navigation. These may include:

- **Neighborhood opposition:** Addressing concerns and objections from neighboring property owners, community groups, or other stakeholders
- **Community review boards:** Presenting your project to community review boards, architectural review committees, or other local bodies that oversee development
- **Stormwater management:** Complying with regulations related to stormwater management, including detention ponds, drainage systems, and water quality controls
- **Utilities and road access:** Ensuring that the subdivided parcels have access to essential utilities, such as water, sewage, and electricity, as well as adequate road access

Once you have a grasp of these concepts, you can start looking for potential properties.

Uncovering Hidden Opportunities in Your Area

Identifying subdivision opportunities requires research, analysis, and local market knowledge. You'll first want to analyze market trends and demands. Study local market trends, including population growth, housing demand, and economic development. Identify areas with high demand for housing, commercial space, or other types of development.

Utilizing websites like NAHB, Corelogic (a leading global provider of property information, analytics, and data-enabled solutions), and FRED (Federal Reserve Economic Data) can provide valuable insights and support informed decision-making in the real estate and construction industries. These websites offer economic forecasts, market trends, and industry news and also give you access to valuable data to support business growth.

Your next step is to identify undervalued or underutilized properties with redevelopment potential. Look for lots with unusual shapes, large acreage, or proximity to key infrastructure such as roads, gas lines, sewer lines, and water meters. Properties near amenities like schools, churches, restaurants, and shopping centers are especially attractive. Start your search using online platforms like Zillow or Redfin, or ask your real estate broker to help identify opportunities through the multiple listing service (MLS).

Once you've found a property, investigate its zoning and utility access. You can usually find this information on your local county tax assessor's website. Understanding the zoning regulations will help you determine if the lot qualifies for subdivision or redevelopment.

Next, evaluate the lot's physical characteristics. Topography, soil quality, and environmental features all impact buildability, accessibility, and compliance with local codes. For added efficiency, build relationships with local real estate professionals, developers, and municipal officials. Attending community planning meetings and zoning commission hearings can also provide valuable insights and connections.

To streamline your research, use online tools like geographic information system (GIS) maps to analyze lot boundaries, zoning, and land use. Public records, including property tax data and ownership history, can offer further context on a property's potential.

Once you've identified a potential subdivision opportunity, conduct a feasibility study to assess the project's viability. Evaluate the costs, risks, and potential returns on investment to determine whether the project is worthwhile. Once you complete this, you'll know whether you should pursue the property.

By following these steps, you can identify potential subdivision opportunities and make informed decisions about which projects to pursue.

Offering and Closing the Lot

My advice is to work with a broker to acquire a property like this. They will have lots of knowledge and experience and are usually up to date on the latest legal issues, which can make for a smooth process. Typically, you would have a feasibility period of thirty to sixty days where you can gather all of the information (discussed in the previous section). Once that has been satisfied, you can move on to the closing period. During closing, you'll need to get your financing together (the funding options for this type of project are listed in depth later on in this chapter).

Once the funding is approved, the acquisition is funded and you close on the property. At this point, you and your architect/builder can begin the process of evaluating the plan for the property.

You've Secured a Lot. Now What?

Once you've secured your lot and are ready to move forward, you'll embark on a complex, multistep journey to reach the final plat. Each stage demands meticulous attention to detail, specific tasks, and regulatory approvals.

To ensure a smooth and efficient process, I strongly advise partnering with a reputable land surveying and civil engineering company. These experts will help you navigate the intricacies of subdivision development, saving you time, money, and potential headaches. A simple online search should yield a list of qualified firms in your local market, allowing you to find the perfect partner for your project.

The Subdivision Process

Here's an overview of the six-phase process I have successfully used. Over time, you may develop your own process—one that might be shorter or longer.

Phase 1: Mapping It Out—Boundary and Topographic Surveys

The boundary and topographic survey is the initial phase of a development project, involving a comprehensive survey to establish property boundaries and identify topographic features. This critical step defines property lines, corners, and edges, ensuring accurate ownership and development, while also mapping natural and man-made features such as elevations, slopes, water bodies, vegetation, and existing infrastructure.

The survey data collected during this phase will inform:

- Site planning and design.
- Grading and excavation plans.
- Stormwater management and drainage systems.
- Environmental impact assessments.
- Permitting and regulatory compliance.

A thorough boundary and topographic survey ensures that the development project begins with accurate and reliable data, minimizing potential errors, delays, and cost overruns.

Phase 2: Preliminary Plans—Submitting Your Short Plat Application

Short platting is the process of dividing a parcel of land into a small number of lots, usually four or fewer, using a simplified legal procedure called a "short plat." This method streamlines the subdivision process compared to standard platting, which allows for more lots. Short platting is often used to divide property among family members or to create a few smaller lots for development.

The preliminary short plat application is a crucial step in the development process, where a proposal is submitted to local authorities for review and approval. This phase involves:

- **Gathering required documents:** Collect and prepare all necessary documents, including:
  - Property deed
  - Survey maps
  - Zoning and land-use information
  - Environmental reports (if required)
- **Preliminary plat mapping:** Create a plat map that illustrates the proposed development, including:
  - Property boundaries
  - Lot lines
  - Streets and alleys
  - Utility locations
  - Environmental features (e.g., wetlands, bodies of water)
- **Development planning:** Outline the proposed development plan, including:
  - Number and type of units (residential, commercial)
  - Density and intensity of development
  - Parking and circulation plans
  - Open space and landscaping proposals

The application is then submitted, then reviewed by local authorities for compliance with zoning ordinances and regulations, and may involve public notification to adjacent property owners and stakeholders. Upon approval, conditional approval, or denial, revisions may be necessary before proceeding with the final plat application, which involves more detailed design and engineering work.

Phase 3: Engineering Excellence—Designing Your Subdivision

During plat engineering, developers and engineers transform the initial design into a detailed, engineered plan, making it a critical phase of the development process. This phase involves:

- **Lot layout:** Design the layout of individual lots, considering factors like size, shape, and orientation
- **Road design:** Engineer the road network, including:
  - Road geometry and alignment
  - Pavement design and materials
  - Drainage and stormwater management
- **Utility planning:** Design and engineer the utility infrastructure, including:
  - Water and sewer systems
  - Electrical and gas distribution
  - Telecommunications and fiber-optic networks
- **Grading and drainage:** Develop a grading plan to ensure proper drainage and stormwater management
- **Erosion and sediment control:** Design measures to prevent erosion and sedimentation during construction.

The phase also involves obtaining necessary permits, complying with regulations, and ensuring that the design meets local, state, and federal requirements, ultimately resulting in a detailed, engineered plan ready for construction.

Phase 4: Staking Your Claim—Construction Staking and Site Prep

In this phase, surveyors physically mark the engineered plat design on the ground during construction staking, providing a visual representation of the proposed development. This phase involves:

- **Physical staking:** Installing stakes and flags to mark the boundaries of lots, roads, utilities, and other infrastructure
- **Reference points:** Establishing reference points to ensure accurate placement of stakes and flags
- **Verification:** Verifying the accuracy of the staking against the engineered plat design

- **Clearing and grading:** Clearing vegetation and debris, and grading the land to prepare it for construction

By physically marking the plat design, construction staking creates a tangible representation of the proposed development. This process helps stakeholders visualize the layout, allows contractors to verify accuracy before breaking ground, and ensures construction aligns with the engineered plan. As a result, projects run more efficiently, with fewer errors and delays.

Phase 5: The Final Touches—As-Builts and Project Closeout

The final phase of the development process involves documenting the construction process, preparing "as-built" plans, and obtaining final inspections and approvals. This phase includes:

- **As-built plans:** Creating detailed plans that reflect the final, built-out state of the project, including any changes or modifications made during construction
- **Documentation:** Compiling records of the construction process, including photos, videos, and written reports
- **Final inspections:** Scheduling final inspections with local authorities to ensure compliance with building codes and regulations
- **Obtaining approvals:** Securing final approvals and certifications from local authorities, including occupancy permits and certificates of completion
- **Project closeout:** Formalizing the completion of the project, including releasing liens, terminating contracts, and transferring ownership

By completing this phase, you'll have a comprehensive record of the project, ensuring that all aspects of the development are properly documented and approved and that the project is formally closed out.

Phase 6: The Grand Finale—Final Plat Approval

The final plat phase of this process involves preparing and submitting the final plat for approval, which includes all necessary documentation, certifications, and approvals. This phase marks the culmination of the development process.

- **Final plat map:** A final plat map is created, reflecting the as-built conditions of the project, including all lots, roads, utilities, and other infrastructure
- **Necessary documentation:** All necessary documentation, including certifications and approvals, is compiled and submitted with the final plat
- **HOA creation (if applicable):** In some states, the creation of an HOA may be required, which involves drafting governing documents, such as bylaws and CC&Rs (covenants, conditions, and restrictions). This is an important step that most first-time developers wouldn't know to do! You can hire a land-use attorney to help you set up the HOA.
- **Final approvals:** The final plat is submitted to local authorities for final approval, ensuring compliance with all regulations and ordinances.
- **Recording the final plat:** Once approved, the final plat is recorded with the county recorder's office, providing public notice of the development.

By completing the final plat phase, you'll have formally completed the development process, and the project will be ready for final inspections, occupancy, and sale.

Funding Your Subdivision Project and Maximizing ROI

Financing a subdivision can be a complex process. There are various funding options available, including loans and partnerships, to make it easier for developers to secure the financing they need.

- **Construction loan:** A short-term loan (usually one to three years) that covers the costs of land acquisition, infrastructure development, and construction
- **Land development loan:** A loan specifically designed for land development, which can include costs such as grading, utilities, and road construction
- **Lot financing:** A loan that allows developers to finance individual lots within the subdivision, often with a partial lien release

- **Joint venture (JV) partnership:** A partnership between the developer and an investor, where the investor provides funding in exchange for a share of the profits
- **Private money lending:** Short-term, high-interest loans from private investors, often used for smaller subdivisions or infill projects
- **Hard-money lending:** Similar to private money lending but often with more stringent requirements and higher interest rates
- **Bank financing:** Traditional bank loans, which may offer more favorable terms but often require more stringent qualifications
- **Mezzanine financing:** Subordinate financing that can be used in conjunction with senior construction loans to provide additional funding

Consider the following factors when choosing a financing option.

- **Interest rates:** Compare rates among different lenders and options
- **Fees:** Consider origination fees, closing costs, and other expenses
- **Repayment terms:** Understand the loan duration, payment schedule, and any prepayment penalties
- **Collateral requirements:** Determine what assets will be used as collateral
- **Credit requirements:** Check the lender's credit score requirements
- **Flexibility:** Consider the lender's willingness to accommodate changes in the project

It's essential to consult with a financial advisor, attorney, and other experts to determine the best financing strategy for your specific subdivision project. My lenders have been incredible resources too. If you can find an investor-friendly lender, someone who has subdivided properties themselves—you've hit the jackpot!

Don't DIY a Lot Subdivision

The story I shared at the beginning of this chapter was my first foray into subdividing a lot, and I was navigating uncharted territory. There were many aspects I didn't fully grasp or anticipate. I was fortunate to find a local land-use specialist who knew the ropes. He'd done this a dozen times before and had great connections with the city officials and permit techs. His consulting fee was pretty steep, but it was worth it for me since I was new to the land subdivision game and needed all the guidance I could get. And the profit I made at the end made it very much worth the investment. I've done three more subdivision projects since then, and I've made sure to work with similar experts on each one.

This is the best advice I can give you for this type of project: To ensure a smooth process, it's crucial to team up with experienced professionals who can guide you through the complexities of subdividing a lot.

Here's a rundown of the experts I recommend having on your team.

- Land-use consultants
- Short plat engineers
- Earthworks and horizontal construction specialists
- Utility specialists (gas, electricity, sewer)
- Land-use attorneys
- Arborists
- HOA/condo attorneys
- Surveyors
- Construction lenders

Now that you've gotten to look at all the parts of the process, let's take a deeper look at my lot subdivision project from beginning to end. No matter where you are in your current journey, there's something to be learned from this example.

For those of you who are experiential learners, the following are two case studies that explore two steps in the process: a) the work that needs to be done to decide whether to purchase the property and b) what a subdivision development project looks like after you've purchased the property.

Case Study: Finding Your Optimal Balance of Effort and Return

I once owned a raw piece of land. As I started doing my feasibility study, I realized that I had two options.

Option 1: I could develop this land until I reached its highest and best potential, which would be to subdivide it and develop three structures: a luxurious primary residence with an attached dwelling unit, and a separate detached dwelling unit. By maximizing the land's potential, I could create a unique and valuable property.

Option 2: I could just sell the land and make money now.

Let's look at each scenario and evaluate returns.

If I decided to pursue development, my first step would be to complete a comprehensive set of feasibility studies. Given that the land was vacant, I would need to conduct several critical surveys, including a geotechnical analysis to assess the soil conditions and stability, an arborist report to evaluate the health and potential impact of existing trees, and a few utility surveys to identify and map existing infrastructure, such as power lines, water pipes, and sewage systems. These studies would provide invaluable insights, which would help me understand the site's constraints and opportunities and overall inform my development strategy.

With the feasibility studies complete, the next phase would involve collaborating with an architect to design the luxury structures, carefully crafting every detail to maximize the property's potential.

Once the design is finalized, I would submit the plans for permitting, a process that typically takes around twelve to fifteen months. This waiting period allows local authorities to review and approve the project, ensuring compliance with regulations and zoning laws.

After securing the necessary permits, the real construction work would begin. This phase would involve bringing in essential utilities, such as electricity, water, and sewage, followed by the actual building of the structures. This construction process would likely take an additional nine to twelve months, depending on factors like weather, labor availability, and material delivery.

From feasibility studies to permit approvals, and finally, to construction completion, the entire development process would span a minimum of two and a half years.

To better understand the financial implications of this project, let's review the scope of the development.

- A 2,500-square-foot SFH
- A 1,000-square-foot adult family home (AFH)
- A 1,000-square-foot DADU

The total livable area would be approximately 4,500 square feet.

Based on the scope of the project, here's a breakdown of the estimated costs.

- **Land cost:** $400,000
- **Construction costs:** Approximately $300 per square foot x 4,500 square feet = $1,350,000
- **Permitting costs and feasibility fees:** Approximately $150,000
- **Construction loan:** $1,350,000 (development costs) x 10% = $135,000

Total estimated cost for the land, financing, and development costs would be $2,035,000.

Now that we've outlined the development costs, let's explore the potential after-build value of the project. After researching new construction comps in the area, we can assume that we should be able to sell the built homes for $650 per square foot.

With that in mind, we can calculate the potential value of each property.

- **2,500-square-foot SFH:** $650/square foot x 2,500 square feet = $1,625,000
- **1,000-square-foot AFH:** $650/square foot x 1,000 square feet = $650,000
- **1,000-square-foot DADU:** $650/square foot x 1,000 square feet = $650,000

Total estimated after-build value: $1,625,000 + $650,000 + $650,000 = $2,925,000.

Next, let's look at the selling costs associated with listing and selling these units. To calculate the total costs associated with selling the properties, let's consider the following expenses.

- **Real estate commission:** Typically 5–6 percent of the sales price
- **Transfer taxes:** Vary by location, but it's safe to assume 1–2 percent of the sales price
- **Insurance and other closing costs:** Approximately 1–2 percent of the sales price

Based on these estimates, here are the calculated selling costs.

- **2,500-square-foot SFH:** $1,625,000 x 8–10% = $130,000–$162,500
- **1,000-square-foot AFH:** $650,000 x 8–10% = $52,000–$65,000
- **1,000-square-foot DADU:** $650,000 x 8–10% = $52,000–$65,000

Total estimated selling costs: $234,000–$292,500

Now that we have *all* of our numbers, let's look at the profit I would make *if* I went ahead and developed this land.

Total Development Costs and Land Value
- **Total development costs:** 4,500 square feet x $300/square foot = $1,350,000
- **Permitting costs:** $150,000
- **Land value:** $400,000
- **Construction loan:** $1,500,000 (development costs) x 10% = $150,000
- **Total costs:** $2,050,000

Selling Costs
- **2,500-square-foot SFH:** $1,625,000 x 8–10% = $130,000–$162,500
- **1,000-square-foot AFH:** $650,000 x 8–10% = $52,000–$65,000

- **1,000-square-foot DADU:** $650,000 x 8–10% = $52,000–$65,000
- **Total estimated selling costs:** $234,000–$292,500

Total Costs and Estimated Profit
- **Total costs:** $2,050,000 (investment + financing) + $234,000-$292,500 (selling costs) = $2,284,000-$2,342,500
- **Total estimated revenue:** $2,925,000
- **Estimated profit:** $2,925,000 - $2,284,000 = $641,000 (best-case scenario)
- **Estimated profit:** $2,925,000 - $2,342,500 = $582,500 (worst-case scenario)

After two and a half years of significant effort and risk, the potential best-case profit is $641,000. However, selling the land as is would yield $400,000 immediately. This raises important questions: Is the potential profit worth the time, effort, and risk involved in the development project? Could the $400,000 from selling the land be invested elsewhere to generate a similar or better return with less risk and effort?

These considerations emphasize the importance of carefully weighing the potential rewards against the costs and risks involved in any development project.

By applying this rigorous analysis to various projects, you can identify potential pitfalls and opportunities, assess risks and rewards, and develop informed strategies to mitigate risks and maximize returns.

The previous case study showcased the work that needs to be done in the decision-making process. So, what happens when you've made the decision to purchase a property?

Case Study: A Three-Lot Subdivision Success Story in Sammamish, Washington

Project Overview
- Purchased an SFH for $525,000
- **Location:** Sammamish, Washington

- **Project type:** Three-Lot Subdivision
- **Project duration:** Four years
- **Project scope:** Remodel the existing house and subdivide the lot into three separate tax parcels
- Complete horizontal construction, including utilities, curbs, and sidewalks for the two new lots

Project Timeline

Year 1:

- Existing house:
  - Renovated the existing house
  - Found a tenant and was able to cover my mortgage and holding costs for the whole lot
  - Costs: $75,000
- Lot subdivision:
  - Planning and Permitting
    - Initiated project planning and permitting process
    - Worked with local authorities to obtain necessary approvals
    - Costs: $125,000 (permitting, consulting fees)

Year 2: Short Platting

- Completed short platting process, dividing the land into three individual lots
- Obtained final approval from local authorities
- Costs: $75,000 (surveying, platting fees)

Years 3–4: Horizontal Construction

- Undertook horizontal construction, including:
  - Installing utilities (water, sewer, electricity).
  - Building curbs and sidewalks.
  - Grading and paving roads.
- Coordinated with contractors and suppliers to ensure timely completion
- Costs: $120,000 (construction costs, materials, labor)

Year 4: Final Plat

- Got all three lots approved and got three separate tax parcel numbers

- Created the HOA
- Sold the house and both lots to three different buyers

Total cost of the project: $920,000
Final sales price: $1,950,000 for all three combined
Total profit made: $1,020,000

Challenges and Lessons Learned

This massive win didn't come for free, nor did it come without challenges. Hopefully you can vicariously take advantage of the lessons I learned so you can do better with your own project!

- **Regulatory hurdles:** Navigating the complex permitting and approval process was a significant challenge. Building relationships with local authorities and staying up to date on regulatory requirements helped mitigate this issue. During my project, the city of Sammamish had a six-month moratorium at this time where they stopped doing any work in the city, thereby delaying the process even more.
- **Construction delays:** Inclement weather and contractor availability issues caused delays in the horizontal construction phase. Implementing a contingency plan and maintaining open communication with contractors helped minimize the impact of these delays.
- **Budget management:** Managing the project budget was crucial to ensuring profitability. Regularly reviewing expenses, getting multiple bids, and making adjustments as needed helped stay on track.

To Subdivide or Not

Lot subdivision projects offer a range of possibilities, from simply subdividing the land to undertaking a full-scale development, including building homes. The level of involvement directly impacts potential earnings: The more you invest in the project, the higher your potential returns.

The three-lot subdivision project in Sammamish, Washington was a complex and time-consuming endeavor. However, through careful planning, perseverance, and a commitment to quality, the project was successfully completed. The experience gained from this project will be invaluable in future development endeavors. I hope you've learned a lot from this chapter too. Before I let you move on, however, here are a few more lessons I want you to learn.

Weighing the Pros and Cons

Subdividing a property can be a lucrative venture, offering the potential for significant profit and valuable development experience. By creating multiple buildable lots or parcels, you can increase the property's overall value and sell the individual parcels for a substantial gain. This process also provides an opportunity to shape the community and contribute to its growth and character. Additionally, working on a subdivision project helps you develop expertise in navigating complex zoning and code regulations, managing development processes, and collaborating with local government agencies.

However, subdividing a property is a complex and time-consuming process that requires significant effort, specialized knowledge, and up-front investments. You'll need to research and comply with local regulations, prepare and submit plans, and negotiate with government agencies, all while managing potential risks and unexpected issues. The process can be affected by environmental concerns, neighboring opposition, or changes in local regulations, making it essential to carefully weigh the pros and cons before deciding to subdivide. Ultimately, success in subdivision requires a deep understanding of local laws, regulations, and development processes, as well as the ability to manage complex projects and mitigate potential risks.

So how does this apply to you and your investment goals? Let's revisit our characters and see how lot subdivision can benefit any real estate investor.

NEW-TO-THE-GAME NOAH

What I want you to take away from this chapter is to learn to spot hidden opportunities. Realize that knowledge is power. Just as I spotted the potential for subdivision by noticing the neighbor's land-use sign, you need to learn to stay curious, research deeply, and educate yourself to uncover opportunities others might miss. This is one powerful way you will be able to level up your newbie status and grow as an investor.

ACTIVE ALEX

Know that persistence pays off, even in the face of challenges. Based on your personality and portfolio style, I know you are used to managing multiple projects. I know that you know it isn't always easy, but the lesson I want you to learn from this chapter is that perseverance through grueling permitting processes, regulatory delays, and community resistance can lead to big rewards. Let this chapter reinforce your resilience to navigating obstacles, because they are worth the effort.

PIVOT PEYTON

What I want you to learn is that building the right team makes all the difference. As you transition into new types of investments, or from one type of investment to another, the lesson is clear: Success in complex projects like subdivisions hinges on collaborating with skilled professionals. From land-use consultants to engineers, leaning into their areas of expertise will cut down not only your learning curve but your project timelines. Leveraging others' expertise reduces risk and accelerates success.

SEASONED-INVESTOR SAM

Stay adaptable and refine your systems. I know you already have a ton of experience in real estate. You might feel like you've learned all the lessons you need to learn. (Or not . . . because you are reading this book!) But from this chapter I want you to take away the importance of staying current with local market trends, zoning laws, and best practices. Even as an expert, I want you to see the value in continually evolving strategies to achieve even greater success.

LONG-GAME LOGAN

The lesson for you in this chapter is to think long term and plan for contingencies. You are used to thriving off sustainable growth, but subdivision might test your patience and require a longer-range vision plan than even *you* aren't used to. The four-year timeline and the unexpected moratorium highlight the importance of preparing for extended timelines and unforeseen hurdles. If you choose to travel down the subdivision road, remind yourself that these projects require patience, financial buffers, and contingency planning. They aren't as straightforward as many of the deals you are used to working with, but if you put in the time and planning, they can become the gem of your property portfolio.

Conclusion to Part 3

Throughout this section, we've explored four powerful strategies for adding value to your real estate investments: sweat equity, refinancing, income-producing units, and subdivision. Each of these approaches offers a unique set of benefits and challenges, but they all share a common goal: to unlock hidden value and maximize returns.

By applying these value-add strategies, you can transform under-performing properties into thriving investments, increase cash flow, and build long-term wealth. Whether you're a seasoned investor or just starting out, these creative approaches can help you stay ahead of the curve and achieve success in the competitive world of real estate investing.

Remember, value-add investing is not just about buying and holding; it's about actively creating value through hard work, creativity, and a willingness to take calculated risks. By embracing this mindset and leveraging the strategies outlined in this section, you'll be well on your way to achieving your investment goals and building a prosperous future.

PART FOUR

The Ultimate Exit—Selling Your Property

If I could go back to the beginning, there's one thing I'd do differently—and it's something I've been asked about more times than I can count.

In those early days, every property I bought felt like a big win. But just as quickly, I often had to sell to free up cash, keep things moving, and generate the active income I needed to stay afloat. At the time, it felt like the right move—and in many ways, it was.

But looking back? I wish I had held on to every single one.

The appreciation, the cash flow, the long-term value—those early properties were the foundation I didn't yet realize I was building. The challenge is, when you're starting out, you're juggling survival and strategy. And survival usually wins.

Still, it's a lesson I carry with me today: Play the long game whenever you can.

That said, if generating income is your immediate priority, it might be time to consider the ultimate exit strategy: selling your property. Whether you're looking to unlock capital, shift into a new investment, or simply realize gains, a successful sale demands thoughtful planning, strategic decisions, and a solid grasp of market dynamics.

In this chapter, we'll explore the essential factors, proven tactics, and best practices to help you maximize your return and execute a smooth, profitable exit.

In Parts 1–3, we learned how to acquire properties, optimize them creatively, and add real value. Now it's time to cash in on those efforts. Whether you want to sell, flip, or trade up, this section gives you the tools to do it right—and do it profitably.

Chapter 10

Flip Frenzy—Mastering the Art of Fix-and-Flip

When I first ventured into real estate investing, I was on a tight deadline. Leaving behind a full-time career meant I had to quickly learn the ropes and generate income. At the time, I briefly considered other real estate careers, like wholesaling or brokering, but quickly picked investing. I made this choice for two main reasons. First, because I wanted to be my own boss and in control of my own time. Second, I knew that as an investor, a single transaction could bring in money equal to an entire year's salary in my former career, so I only needed one project to come together before my savings ran out.

Through a bit of research, I learned that the market for fix-and-flips seemed likely to be my best bet at meeting both of these criteria.

A fix-and-flip project is a type of real estate investment strategy that involves:

- **Buying a distressed property:** Purchasing a property that needs repairs, renovations, or rehabilitation, often at a discounted price below market value given its condition
- **Renovating the property:** Making necessary repairs, upgrades, and improvements to increase the property's value and appeal
- **Selling the property for profit:** Selling the renovated property at a higher price than the original purchase price, earning a profit from the difference

Renovations differ significantly depending on whether you're flipping a property for resale or holding onto it as a rental investment. Renovations for rental properties emphasize functionality and durability, incorporating features that reduce operating costs, attract tenants, and increase long-term value appreciation.

In contrast, for fix-and-flip projects, the focus is on updates that appeal to potential buyers, creating meaningful, versatile floor plans, and prioritizing popular design trends to maximize resale value.

Flipping homes is a very challenging type of real estate investment, in my opinion. With tight deadlines and razor-thin margins, even the slightest misstep can be costly. I actually lost money on my very first flip! So why did I start there—and why do I still continue flipping properties even today? The answer is simple: When executed correctly, house flipping can be incredibly lucrative. One of my most notable successes was a house I flipped in less than five months for a generous profit of $225,000.

Fix-and-flip projects can range from minor cosmetic updates to full-scale renovations, depending on the property's condition and the investor's goals. I've found that cosmetic renovations are riskier than full-gut renovations due to their lower profit margins. In contrast, full-gut distressed properties are typically offered at steeper discounts, providing a more significant buffer for errors, market fluctuations, and unexpected setbacks—and more money left over when they're sold for a much higher price. Even though the larger-scale projects can seem scarier, they are actually less risky in the long run.

For a comprehensive guide to navigating the fix-and-flip life cycle, I highly recommend *The House Flipping Framework* by my good friend and mentor James Dainard (www.BiggerPockets.com/ReadHouse Flipping). This invaluable resource provides a step-by-step road map for executing each stage of the process.

The Life Cycle of a Fix-And-Flip Property

The typical life cycle of a fix-and-flip project can be broken down into the following steps.

1. **Buying criteria:** Defining the investment strategy and identifying the ideal property
2. **Deal finding:** Locating potential properties that meet the buying criteria
3. **Underwriting:** Analyzing the property's financials to determine its potential for profit
4. **Deal financing:** Securing funding for the project
5. **Rehab process:** Executing the renovation plan
6. **Sale:** Listing the property to sell

It is essential to understand this whole life cycle because a break in any one of these stages can lead to an expensive mistake, potentially derailing the entire project and eliminating profits.

Deal or No Deal: Establishing Your Buying Criteria

In the beginning, I took on every project that came my way, but by my second year, I had discovered a crucial truth: Quality surpasses quantity. Concentrating on fewer, higher-potential flips generated superior results compared to rushing through low-margin projects. As my business grew, I fine-tuned my buying strategy through trial and error. If you're still unsure about your strategy, don't worry—sometimes you need to dive in and experiment with a few projects to figure it out, just like I did.

To illustrate my point. Here's a glimpse of my buying criteria during my first year.

- Crappy houses in good, desirable, neighborhoods
- Acquisition price under $300,000 for fix-and-flip
- Prefer houses that are two-thirds of the median price point (not luxury)
- Single-family houses, prefer two to five bedrooms and one to four bathrooms
- Location: Puget Sound Metro. High-demand areas where my projects would sell fast, and nothing rural
- Condition: Prefer cosmetic fixers
- Year built: 1965 and newer
- Profit goal: 15 percent cash-on-cash returns on purchase price plus improvements
- Must have at least $40,000 profit (after *all* expenses: agent's commission, cost of money, closing costs etc.)

In my second year, I completed eight flips, generating a total profit of $118,000. However, the reality was that I spent countless hours chasing down deals, managing contractors, and dealing with returns—all for a relatively modest profit. It was a valuable lesson in the importance of scaling efficiently and prioritizing high-margin deals.

I shifted my strategy to focus on buying homes with:

- Higher profit potential (minimum 15 percent cash-on-cash return).
- Functional and appealing floor plans.
- Desirable locations: (i.e., good school districts and attractive neighborhoods)
- Favorable land characteristics: Flat lots and easy access
- Key features: At least three bedrooms and one and a half bathrooms
- Pricing: Below two-thirds of the median price point

I avoided homes with:

- Unappealing physical characteristics: low basements, dead spaces
- Undesirable locations (i.e., ugly neighboring properties and busy streets)
- Restrictive or high-maintenance properties:
  - Condos and townhomes with strict rules
  - Jurisdictions with difficult permitting processes

With new criteria, the following year, I scaled back to just two fix-and-flip deals, but the results were staggering—a profit of $240,000. This experience was eye-opening, as I realized that focusing on quality over quantity allowed me to:

- Enjoy the process more.
- Work with top-notch contractors.
- Design better floor plans.
- Create homes that were in demand so I could generate multiple offers.

It was a pivotal moment that shifted my approach to fix-and-flipping, and I've never looked back. By year three, I had only one criterion: deals with a profit spread over $100,000.

It is important to consider all the factors and create a buying criterion that is tailored to your local market, skills, budget, and risk tolerance. Build a buying criteria that can withstand market volatility.

I highly recommend taking some time to assess your strengths, weaknesses, and what's happening in your market. This will help you identify properties that are a great fit for you and, ultimately, lead to more profitable and less stress.

Finding the Hidden Gems

While it can be easy to find one deal here and there, scaling your house-flipping business requires a consistent deal-flow pipeline. This involves directly contacting sellers to find off-market properties as well as networking with wholesalers, agents, and fellow investors. After you get your feet wet and have a bit of investment experience, I recommend getting your broker's license to take down on-market deals.

Over the years, I've discovered deals through various creative channels.

- Wholesalers
- Online marketplaces: Craigslist, social media posts
- Networking:
  - Meetups
  - Virtual events
  - Neighbors of my flip properties
  - Open houses
- Local advertising: Flyers
- Online communities: Facebook groups

Rather than simply rely on the MLS, these unconventional methods have helped me stay ahead of the competition and find hidden gems in the market. In fact, one of my most memorable deals came from an unexpected referral. The seller of one of my flip projects introduced me to his 80-year-old friend Greg, who was looking to downsize from his distressed house to a mobile home. This personal connection led to a win-win deal, and I ended up buying Greg's house too!

Let me walk you through my process to finding fix-and-flip deals. First, identify markets that have demand for upgraded properties and then identify specific properties in that area that will yield massive returns once upgraded. Here are some key characteristics to look for when identifying value-add properties.

- **Location:** Always pick high-demand neighborhoods with good access to schools and amenities. I avoid busy streets and homes on roads with double yellow lines.
- **Lot size:** larger lots are a bonus
- **Parking:** I prefer properties with attached garages or space to build one
- **Floor plans:** I like having a meaningful floor plan to work with. It's harder to renovate tight spaces, short basements, low ceiling heights.
- **Neighbors:** Renovating homes surrounded by good neighboring properties can yield higher values even if the subject property itself is smaller. A good rule of thumb to follow is always buy the worst home on the block.
- **Bedroom/bathroom count:** You can add more later, but I try to choose properties that have at least two to three bedrooms and at least two bathrooms
- **Zoning:** Buying properties that can be rezoned to increase density can be very lucrative
- Total square footage including unfinished spaces (like basements) and unused rooms (like garages, bonus rooms, etc.) that can be turned into livable spaces

Here's a step-by-step guide to find these kinds of properties.

1. Research high-demand neighborhoods
   o Look for areas with:
     - Growing population.
     - New developments (commercial or residential).
     - Improving infrastructure.
     - Good schools and amenities.
2. Identify undervalued properties
   o Search for properties with:
     - Low sales prices compared to surrounding homes.
     - Deferred maintenance or needed repairs.
     - Outdated design or functionality.
     - Potential for expansion or renovation.
3. Analyze property characteristics
   o Consider:
     - Lot size and zoning.
     - Parking and garage potential.

- Floor plan and layout.
- Number of bedrooms and bathrooms.
- Potential for adding value through renovations.

4. Find properties that work within your criteria
   - **Direct from seller:** Purchase properties directly from motivated sellers, such as estate sales, divorce, or financial distress
   - **Real estate brokers:** Work with brokers who specialize in off-market or distressed properties to gain access to exclusive listings
   - **Wholesalers:** Partner with wholesalers who find and negotiate deals on your behalf, providing convenience and potential discounts
   - **Auctions:** Attend auctions, both online and offline, to find properties at discounted prices, but be cautious of risks
   - **Referrals from other investors and friends:** Leverage your network to find off-market opportunities through trusted sources
   - **On-market listings:** Search online real estate platforms, such as Zillow or Redfin, to find properties listed for sale
   - **MLS:** Utilize the MLS to access a comprehensive database of properties for sale, including those not publicly listed online

5. Inspect properties and crunch numbers
   - Physically inspect potential properties
   - Run financial projections and analyze potential returns
   - Consider hiring a professional inspector or appraiser

By following these steps, you'll increase your chances of finding properties with potential for forced appreciation. Always remember to conduct thorough research, analyze numbers carefully, and consult with professionals before making a decision.

Once you've identified properties with upside potential, securing financing becomes the next hurdle. While conventional financing is often the preferred route, it's frequently not an option for severely distressed properties.

In fact, approximately 90 percent of the time, conventional financing won't be available for properties in disrepair. However, it's precisely these types of properties that offer the greatest opportunity for value appreciation through renovation.

Here are some alternative financing methods to consider for severely distressed properties.

- **Hard money loans:** Short-term, high-interest loans for fix-and-flip projects or forcing appreciation
- **Private money loans:** Short-term loans from private lenders, often with higher interest rates and lower loan-to-value ratios
- **Partnering with investors:** Partnering with investors to access capital in exchange for equity or a share of profits
- **Home equity lines of credit (HELOCs):** Lines of credit using existing equity in a property you already own, often with lower interest rates and longer repayment terms. I started my real estate business with a HELOC!
- **Cash out refinance:** Refinancing an existing loan and taking out additional cash, often with lower interest rates and longer repayment terms
- **Owner financing:** Always check if the owner can finance the property, as it can be the most cost-effective choice, often featuring lower down payments, flexible terms, and potential for better interest rates. This approach can lead to significant savings and a smoother transaction.

Underwriting Deals for Maximum ROI

Once you've identified a project, accurate underwriting is crucial. Underwriting in real estate is like putting on your detective hat (or accountant's visor) and running the numbers to see if an investment property is worth the leap. It's the art (and science) of analyzing the property's value, repair costs, and income potential to figure out if you're looking at a profitable deal—or one you should walk away from.

Think about underwriting like a seat-belt check—a habit that will keep you safe and something you should do *every* time. This process helps you overlook any big emotions that might be blinding you and help you look at each potential property purchase logically. Does this deal align with your financial goals and make sense on paper? If the numbers don't work, it's a no-go. But if they do, consider it your greenlight and move forward.

Personally, I underwrite five to ten deals before selecting one to pursue. Underwriting a deal comes at no cost, making it a risk-free opportunity to hone your skills. Take advantage of this by underwriting as many deals as possible, which will help you develop a keen eye for spotting potential duds and making informed investment decisions.

The first step in underwriting is to gather the property information. You'll want the following details:

- Property address and location
- Purchase price or potential acquisition cost
- Property type (SFH, condo, etc.)
- Size and layout
- Age and condition
- Zoning and land-use information

Next, you'll want to analyze the market to calculate the property's resale value, or ARV. This involves studying comparable properties, aka "comps," in the area—homes that are similar in size, layout, and features. Key factors to consider include square footage, number of bedrooms and bathrooms, finishes, and amenities. But here's the plot twist in this particular *Choose Your Own Adventure* story: The property's condition matters big-time. Two homes with identical stats can have vastly different values based on their aesthetic appeal. It's like comparing a vintage, avocado-green-kitchened home reminiscent of the Brady Bunch era to a modern, Instagram-worthy smart home à la MTV's *Cribs*.

The "vintage" home, with its outdated decor and retro vibe, might appeal to a niche buyer, but its value will likely be lower. On the other hand, the "modern smart home," with its sleek lines, high-tech features, and stylish design, will likely command a premium price.

To get an accurate ARV, try to find comps that reflect the post-renovation condition you're aiming for with your property. You'll also want to assess the market trends and potential for appreciation.

If you're feeling overwhelmed or unsure, don't sweat it! A trusted real estate agent or investor can be your guide through this process. Their experience and access to market data can help you make informed decisions with confidence.

The next step in the process is cost estimation, which involves accounting for all expenses, including the property purchase price, renovation costs, holding costs (like utilities and insurance), and closing costs. Don't forget closing costs, including escrow and recording costs and any county taxes that may apply as well as any financing costs such as interest and points for the loan term.

After that, it's time to figure out your rehab budget. How much will it cost to upgrade the property? Be sure to include costs for both the supplies and labor. You'll need to:

- Create a detailed scope of work.
- Get bids from contractors or estimate costs using a renovation software.
- Include costs for materials, labor, and permits.
- Consider contingencies for unexpected expenses.

Next, you'll need to calculate the financing costs with the rehab budget in mind. Determine your financing option (hard money, private money, etc.). You'll calculate the interest rate and loan terms, in addition to the points and fees.

The next cost you'll need to consider is the price tag for marketing, which will include staging the property and photography of the space. The amount of money you'll need to spend on these tasks is largely dependent on your location. It will be important to do some research to see common best practices for your regional area. You could spend both too much and too little on this task and completely miss a sale or waste a bunch of cash simply because you didn't understand your buyer and your market. Don't let that be you!

And finally, you'll need to calculate the costs associated with selling the property, including items such as real estate commissions, excise taxes, escrows, and closing fees.

If it sounds like a lot, you're right! Which is why you need to think about it ahead of time, really crunch the numbers, and make a plan that will work out in your favor.

Let's Recap the Underwriting Process

1. **Calculate the ARV:** Study comparable properties in the area, considering factors like square footage, number of bedrooms and bathrooms, finishes, and amenities. Reflect the post-renovation condition you're aiming for with your property.
2. **Estimate costs:** Account for all expenses, including:
   - Property purchase price.
   - Renovation costs.

- Holding costs (utilities, insurance).
- Closing costs (escrow, recording costs, county taxes, financing costs).

3. **Determine rehab budget:** Calculate the cost of upgrading the property, including supplies and labor
4. **Determine marketing costs:** Research and budget for marketing expenses, such as staging and photography, tailored to your regional area
5. **Determine selling costs:** Calculate costs associated with selling the property, including real estate commissions, excise taxes, and closing fees

Calculating Profits and ROI

Now it's time to crunch the numbers and calculate your potential profits. This is the exciting part! It's time to see the potential income you can earn from the property through rental income or resale value.

To calculate your total profit, subtract all the costs (purchase price, renovation costs, holding costs, and selling costs) from the ARV. This will give you a clear picture of your potential profit.

Before moving forward, it's essential to conduct a risk assessment and analysis to identify potential risks, such as:

- Market fluctuations.
- Zoning restrictions.
- Unexpected costs.

By understanding these risks up front, you can make informed decisions and avoid potential pitfalls.

After analyzing the numbers and assessing potential risks, you'll be able to determine your ROI. This will help you decide if the expected profits justify the investment.

To make this process clearer, let's work through an example together. This will help illustrate the concepts and make it easier to apply them to your own real estate investments.

Here is the deal analyzer I use, which I developed ten years ago, after experimenting with various versions from different sources. Since then, it has been my go-to tool for underwriting thousands of properties. While the numbers may change with each new deal, the underlying mechanics have remained remarkably consistent. Over the years, I've refined my deal analyzer to ensure it remains accurate and relevant. Its longevity is a testament to its effectiveness in helping me make informed investment decisions.

Whether you're a seasoned investor or just starting out, a reliable deal analyzer is essential for success. It helps you crunch the numbers, identify potential risks and opportunities, and make informed decisions that drive your investment strategy forward.

Property Values & Pricing		
After Repair Value		$1,640,000
Current "As Is" Value		
Subdivision + repair costs		$200,000
Purchase Price		$1,080,000
Estimated Hold Time (months)		8.0
Purchase & Repair Costs		**$1,280,000**

Financing Costs		Purchase + Rehab
First Mortgage/Lien Amount	85%	$1,088,000
First Mortgage Points	1.25%	$13,600
First Mortgage Annual Interest	10.75%	$116,960
First Mortgage Interest (for holding period)		$77,973
Second Mortgage/Lien Amount	10%	$128,000
Second Mortgage Points	0.00%	$0
Second Mortgage Annual Interest	9.00%	$11,520
Second Mortgage Interest (for holding period)		$7,680
Rehab Loan	0%	$0
Rehab Loan Points	0	$0
Rehab Loan Annual Interest	0.00%	$0
Rehab Loan Interest (for holding period)		$0.00
Miscellaneous Finance Costs-Fees + Draws		$1,500
Total Financing Costs		**$100,753**

Purchase & Deal Analysis		
After Repair Value		$1,640,000
Purchase Price		$1,080,000
Estimated Repair Costs		$200,000
Total Financing Costs		$100,753
Total Holding Costs		$5,000
Total Buying Transaction Costs		$3,000
Total Selling Transaction Costs		$141,168

Hold Costs (Monthly)	Annually	Monthly
Property Taxes	$6,000	$500
HOA & Condo Fees	$0	$0
Insurance Costs	$1,000	$83
Utility Costs (Expandable)	$500	$42
Gas		$0
Water		$0
Electricity		$0
Other		$0
Miscellaneous Holding Costs		$0
Total Monthly Holding Costs		**$625**

Buying Transaction Costs	% of Purchase	Total
Escrow & Title		$1,500
Recording Fees		$1,500
Miscellaneous Buying Costs		$0
Total Buying Transaction Costs		**$3,000**

Selling Transaction Costs	% of ARV	Total
Escrow & Title	1.00%	$16,400
Selling Recording Fees		$0
Realtos Fees	5.00%	$82,000
Transfer & Conveyance Fees	0.12%	$1,968
Home Warranty		$0
Staging Costs		$8,000
Marketing Costs		
Excise Tax	2.00%	$32,800
Total Selling Transaction Costs		**$141,168**

Potential Return & Profit Analysis		
Assumes sale is on or before		5/18/23
Purchase + Repair Estimate Cost Per Sq. Ft		$691.89
Total Out-Of-Pocket		$108,753
Total Amount Borrowed from HELOC		$128,000
ROI (Purhcase+Rehab+Costs-->ARV)		7.20%
ROI (profit/HELOC loan)		101.22%
Net Profit		$110,079

Estimated Net Profit and ROI Snapshot		
Net Profit		**$110,079**
Profit Percentage		**101.22%**

Financing Your Flip with Debt, Equity, and Private Notes

Distressed properties do not qualify for conventional financing. This creates opportunities to get creative!

If you don't want to use up all your cash on a deal, then the most common financing method for real estate deals is through hard-money lenders. These lenders can provide up to 90 percent of the purchase price and cover 100 percent of the rehab costs, making it an attractive option for investors. Seller financing is another great way to go as it doesn't require the same level of underwriting as traditional lenders. Bridge loans also provide temporary financing for six to thirty-six months, allowing investors to acquire and renovate distressed properties before securing long-term financing.

The other way is by raising private money. Here are a few of my favorite, creative ways to do that.

- Leverage your inner circle: friends and family
- Connect with fellow real estate investors in your network
- Target local businesses and organizations

You can also identify real estate groups within industries like tech, medicine, and marketing. As a prime example, Seattle's thriving tech hub has provided me with opportunities to connect with real estate clubs at industry giants like Google, Meta, Amazon, and Microsoft. A real estate club is a group of people who share an interest in real estate and may invest in real estate together. These connections have led to partnerships with many of my private lenders. By delivering a simple yet informative presentation, you can raise awareness about your work and educate potential investors. These high-net-worth individuals often lack the time to invest themselves and seek partnerships with dedicated and driven professionals like yourself, who demonstrate grit and expertise in their field.

My top priority is protecting my investors' funds. I'm proud to say that, with over a decade of experience, I've maintained a flawless track record: Not a single private lender has lost money investing with me.

When investing with other people's money, it's crucial to exercise extreme diligence and fight to protect their funds. While it's not always possible to generate high profits or even break even, it's essential to make every effort to minimize losses and preserve capital.

Speaking of capital, let's dive into that. I typically raise capital through two primary structures: debt and equity.

Debt Financing: Leveraging Loans for Maximum Gain

In a debt arrangement, investors provide funding for a specified term, usually one year, in exchange for a fixed interest rate. Interest payments are typically made on a monthly or quarterly basis or on a balloon payment schedule.

> A balloon payment schedule is a situation in which the investor receives their principal and interest in a lump sum at the end of the loan term.

Equity Financing: Partnering for Profit

In an equity arrangement, investors receive a share of the profits in exchange for their funding. The typical equity stake I offer ranges from 10 to 15 percent, but this can vary depending on the investor's level of involvement. Passive investors usually get around a 10 to 15 percent equity stake, whereas active investors get a higher equity stake, which is negotiable based on their level of participation.

It's essential to note that equity financing carries more risk to the lender (investor), because the investors' returns are directly tied to the project's performance. If the deal incurs losses, investors will also lose money. Therefore, it's crucial to clearly communicate this risk to potential investors.

Additionally, with equity financing, investors typically don't receive any payments until the project is sold, at which point they'll receive their share of the profits.

On the flip side, the potential upside for investors in an equity structure is substantial. I've had deals that generated profits of $200,000 to $300,000 on a single flip, earning my investors significant returns as a result. In one instance, an investor earned nearly $60,000 in just five months on a single deal! This highlights the potential for substantial gains when investing in a profitable project.

Securing Private Notes: Alternative Funding Options

To protect both parties' interests, private notes are used and typically secured through two key documents: a promissory note and a deed of trust.

Promissory Note

A promissory note is a binding agreement between the borrower (you) and the lender (investor). This document outlines the terms of the loan, including:

- The principal amount borrowed,
- Interest rate and payment schedule,
- Repayment terms and maturity date, and
- Any late payment fees or penalties.

By signing a promissory note, you acknowledge your obligation to repay the loan according to the agreed-upon terms.

Deed of Trust

A deed of trust, also known as a trust deed, is a security instrument that grants the lender a lien on a specific property. This document:

- Identifies the property being used as collateral,
- Outlines the lender's rights and interests in the property, and
- Provides a clear path for foreclosure in the event of default.

By recording a deed of trust, the lender gains a secured interest in the property, which can be used to recover their investment if you fail to repay the loan. Together, these two documents provide a robust framework for securing private notes and protecting the interests of both parties involved.

Rehabbing Your Flip

Again, there are many phases within this one step of the process. You can see why it can take a long time for people to get the lay of the land and learn all they need to know to be successful. From designing and budgeting to renovation and construction, there are a lot of things to think about as you work through a property rehab.

Design and Planning

Create a cohesive design

Develop a clear vision for the property's renovation, ensuring a cohesive and appealing design.

Start by defining the theme or style of your house, whether it's contemporary, mid-century, modern, or something else. If this is your first fix-and-flip project, it might be helpful to work with an interior designer for ideas on establishing this overall theme and style. This will serve as a guiding force for selecting finishes that complement and enhance the overall aesthetic. By choosing finishes that align with your home's style, you'll create a cohesive and harmonious space that reflects your vision. Some tips:

- Choose a consistent hardware color throughout the house, including door handles, cabinet pulls, faucets, and bathroom fixtures.
- Select tile, cabinets, vanities, and countertops at the same time to envision how they'll work together once installed.
- Consider the little elements that can elevate the look and feel of your home, such as matching shower doors and bathroom fixtures, accent walls, wainscoting.
- Don't ignore curb appeal. This is huge. I always make sure that the grass outside is green. I invest in fresh sod and cool plants whenever possible. Buyers' first impressions go a long way.

By paying attention to these details, you can create a beautiful and cohesive space that reflects your personal style.

Plan for functionality

When renovating a property, I prioritize functional layouts and amenities that resonate with potential buyers. My go-to strategies include:

- **Open-concept living:** I always remove the walls between the living room and kitchen to create a seamless, open-concept space that fosters socializing and entertainment
- **Primary suite retreat:** I make it a point to create a serene primary suite, complete with a relaxing atmosphere and ample storage
- **Basement transformation:** I transform unfinished basements into inviting spaces by adding a new room,

bathroom, and often, a stylish wet bar—a bonus feature that adds to the property's appeal.

By incorporating these functional design elements, I'm able to create homes that appeal to potential buyers and ultimately drive sales.

Budgeting and Cost Management

Setting a realistic budget is crucial to the success of your flip. A comprehensive budget should account for all expenses, including:

- Purchase price
    - **Acquisition costs:** Include the purchase price, closing costs, and any other fees associated with buying the property
- Renovation costs
    - **Construction costs:** Estimate the costs of materials, labor, and permits required for the renovation
    - **Contingency fund:** Allocate a portion of the budget for unexpected expenses or changes to the original plan. I typically have a 15 percent contingency for every project.
- Holding costs
    - **Mortgage payments:** Calculate the monthly mortgage payments, including interest and principal
    - **Property taxes:** Estimate the annual property taxes and divide by twelve for monthly costs
    - **Insurance:** Include the cost of property insurance, liability insurance, and any other relevant policies
    - **Utilities:** Estimate the monthly utility costs, including electricity, water, gas, and trash removal
- Maintenance
    - Allocate funds for ongoing maintenance and repairs
- Additional expenses
    - **Inspections and appraisals:** Include the costs of inspections, appraisals, and other due diligence expenses
    - **Permits and fees:** Estimate the costs of permits, licenses, and other fees associated with the renovation
    - **Marketing and sales:** Allocate funds for marketing and sales expenses, including real estate agent commissions

- **Staging:** I stage all my properties with furniture, appliances, and decor because it really helps sell them for a much higher value. Staging helps buyers envision what each of the spaces will look and feel like.
- Buffer for unexpected expenses
  - **Emergency fund:** Set aside a portion of the budget for unexpected expenses or changes to the original plan, like not getting permits in a timely manner or needing to hold on to the property for longer periods of time due to poor market conditions.

By accounting for all the possible expenses, you'll be able to establish a realistic budget that sets your project up for success.

Renovation and Construction

Finding and hiring the right contractor can be a daunting task. I learned this lesson firsthand. Over the years, I've undergone a significant evolution in my approach to finding and hiring contractors. Here's a glimpse into my journey.

Before finding my current crew, I worked with eighteen to twenty different contractors. It took time and trial and error, but the process ultimately paid off. I've now partnered with the same crew for seven years.

Connections with contractors and other construction resources are essential for your growth as an investor. Truly, these relationships are the key factor that can make or break your project. While there is no magic wand that ensures you pick a winner every time, there are a few key characteristics I keep my eyes peeled for that help me identify high-quality humans I want to work with. Here are some ways to source contractors.

- **Permit research:** Many municipalities offer online permit databases where you can search for construction permits linked to specific addresses. This can help you track ongoing or completed projects and connect with contractors who may be working in your target areas, as well as pre-identify who might be available sooner rather than later.

- **Neighborhood reconnaissance:** Take a drive through up-and-coming neighborhoods to identify properties being renovated or newly constructed. Pay attention to business logos posted on work trucks and on lawn signs. These "drive-for-dollars" opportunities often lead to discovering contractors active in the area.
- **Investor connections:** Engaging with fellow real estate investors can be a valuable way to obtain trusted contractor referrals. Other investors often have firsthand experience with local professionals and can point you to reliable general contractors and tradespeople (as well as which ones to avoid).
- **Networking events:** Investor meetups are a hotspot for contractors looking for new projects. These events are perfect for networking and establishing connections with both contractors and other investors who may offer recommendations. A win-win!
- **Building supply centers:** Visit your local home improvement or building supply stores, and take the time to introduce yourself to contractors who are shopping for materials. These interactions can lead to useful insights and connections for future projects. It might feel a bit awkward, but hey, you get to walk away in thirty seconds . . . so tough it out and go for it!
- **Supplier referrals:** Many building material suppliers maintain strong relationships with contractors and often offer recommendations to help secure business. Be sure to ask about trusted installers and contractors when you visit these stores.

No matter how you gain and collect names, be sure to keep track of them in an organized fashion, so you can call on them when you are ready.

Partnering with skilled, reliable contractors is crucial to delivering high-quality work on time and within budget. Once you've identified a few contractors you'd might like to work with, here are some tips to help you lock in on the right contractor.

Get referrals

- Ask for recommendations: Ask colleagues, friends, or family members who have completed similar projects for recommendations
- Check online reviews: Look up contractors on review websites like Angie's List, Yelp, or Google Reviews

Verify credentials

- Licenses and certifications: Ensure contractors have the necessary licenses, certifications, and insurance
- Check with the Better Business Bureau: Verify contractors' reputations with the Better Business Bureau

Evaluate experience

- Check portfolios: Review contractors' past projects to ensure they have experience with similar scopes and budgets
- Ask about their team: Ensure contractors have a reliable team in place to complete the project

Get multiple bids

- Compare prices and services: Get bids from at least three contractors to compare prices, services, and timelines
- Evaluate the scope of work: Ensure each contractor's bid includes a detailed scope of work, timeline, and payment terms

Communicate clearly

- Clearly define expectations: Ensure contractors understand your expectations, timelines, and budget
- Establish a communication plan: Set up regular meetings or updates to ensure the project stays on track

Monitor Progress

- Regularly inspect the worksite: This is crucial to ensuring that contractors are meeting their obligations, obtaining necessary permits, and scheduling inspections. These walk-throughs also help ensure that your vision is taking shape and the final product aligns with your original design intent. By catching mistakes or issues early on, you can save time and money in the long run. For instance, correcting errors during the framing stage can be significantly less expensive than if discovered after drywall installation, avoiding costly rework and reducing the risk of project delays and budget overruns.

- Track expenses and payments: Monitor expenses and payments to ensure the project stays within budget

When I first started flipping houses, I didn't know where to begin when it came to finding contractors. I relied on online directories—sites like Thumbtack and Porch and even Craigslist—to find potential candidates. This approach led to a mix of good and bad experiences, with some contractors delivering excellent results while others failed to meet expectations.

I would start each project by collecting bids from seven to ten different contractors. Although this process was tedious, it provided valuable insight into the project's scope and the estimated cost range. This information helped me make informed decisions and set realistic expectations for each renovation.

As I progressed, I started to find other ways to find reliable contractors—I requested referrals while shopping at cabinet stores, tile stores, and home improvement stores like Home Depot. I also frequently tapped into my own network, asking anyone and everyone who they loved working with. I soon realized that the best people to work with came referred to me by other investors who had firsthand experience working with them. These referrals provided a level of trust and confidence in their abilities I couldn't find from an internet search; they were golden.

To this day, I've found that the best contractors are those referred to me by my trusted tradesmen, including electricians, plumbers, and roofers. I make it a point to ask them about their preferred contractors—the ones who pay on time, show up reliably, and communicate effectively. These referrals have consistently led me to contractors with excellent reputations, who ultimately deliver high-quality work. By tapping into my tradesmen's network, I've been able to build a reliable team of contractors who share my commitment to excellence. This approach has saved me time, reduced stress, and ultimately contributed to the success of my flipping business.

Managing Contractors

When working with contractors, proper paperwork is paramount. I require my general contractors to sign the following documents prior to commencing work, even if we've successfully partnered on multiple projects in the past. This consistent approach establishes clear expectations and helps maintain a smooth process for every project.

- **Contract agreement:** A comprehensive contract outlining the scope of work, payment terms, timeline, and responsibilities of both parties
- **Scope of work (SOW):** A detailed document describing the specific tasks, materials, and services to be provided by the contractor. Clearly outline the project's objectives, specifications, and design plans to ensure both you and the contractor have a mutual understanding of the project's requirements. Have this plan written and shared in a place that is easy to access by both of you
- **Payment terms and schedule:** A document specifying the payment amounts, due dates, and methods
- **Change order agreement:** A document outlining the process for making changes to the original scope of work, including pricing and approval procedures
- **Warranty and liability:** A document specifying the contractor's warranty and liability obligations, including the duration of the warranty and the extent of their liability
- **Insurance and bonding:** Proof of the contractor's insurance and bonding, including workers' compensation, liability insurance, and any required licenses
- **Lien waivers:** A document waiving the contractor's right to file a lien against your property in exchange for payment
- **Permitting and compliance:** Documentation confirming the contractor's responsibility for obtaining necessary permits and complying with local regulations
- **Termination clause:** A document outlining the conditions under which the contract can be terminated, including notice periods and penalties

Having these documents signed will help prevent misunderstandings, ensure compliance with regulations, and protect your interests throughout the project.

Next, you'll want to prepare the jobsite with access and documentation. Ensure the jobsite is properly set up for the contractor, with all required permits, paperwork, and access points clearly defined. This will allow work to begin ASAP rather than experiencing delays right from the start.

As the renovation progresses, conduct weekly walk-through and document progress. Perform regular site walk-throughs to monitor progress, taking detailed notes and photos. Keep track of the project's budget, status, and any issues that may arise, ensuring everything is on schedule. If troubles arise, make sure to communicate with the contractor both clearly and quickly.

Staging for Success

Once you are done renovating the property, it is now time to sell! To maximize your selling price, it's imperative to present your flip in the best possible light.

Staging is a crucial step in showcasing a property's potential, and the statistics are compelling—in my personal experience, staged homes typically sell faster than their un-staged counterparts because it gives the buyer a vision for what the home can look like. They can begin to envision themself in the space. I swear by the power of staging, using a professional stager on every single one of my projects. Even when renovating multifamily properties, I stage at least one unit to give future tenants a glimpse into the possibilities. By staging your properties, you're not only highlighting the functionality of each space but also helping buyers or tenants envision how to maximize the use of smaller areas, making the property feel more livable and desirable.

How to Wow Potential Buyers

- **Neutral color palette:** A neutral color scheme to appeal to a wide range of buyers
- **Minimal clutter:** A clutter-free space to create a sense of openness and flow
- **Furniture placement:** Strategic furniture placement to create a sense of functionality and flow
- **Lighting:** Proper lighting to highlight the best features of the space
- **Accent decor:** Thoughtful use of accent decor, such as artwork, rugs, and accessories, to add visual interest

- **Outdoor spaces:** Inviting outdoor spaces, such as patios or decks, to expand the living area
- **Highlighting best features:** Staging that highlights the best features of the property, such as a fireplace or stunning views

Avoid These Deal-Killing Mistakes

- **Over-accessorizing:** Too many accessories or clutter can make a space feel overwhelming
- **Poor lighting:** Insufficient or harsh lighting can make a space feel uninviting
- **Inconsistent style:** A mix of styles or periods can create a confusing and unappealing space
- **Lack of functionality:** Staging that ignores the functionality of a space can make it feel impractical

Another important aspect to complete before putting your house in front of the public is updating the landscaping. A well-manicured lawn and beautifully landscaped yard can cement a positive first impression in the buyer's mind.

I'll never forget the time I renovated a million-dollar property and made the mistake of leaving the yard unfinished. Despite the house being perfectly situated in the middle of a huge and picturesque lot, I decided to cut costs and leave the landscaping as is. I figured it would save me some money, especially since I was already over budget.

However, this decision proved to be a costly mistake. For two whole months, the property sat on the market with no offers, racking up hefty holding costs that far exceeded what I would have spent on landscaping. It wasn't until my broker advised me to invest in some landscaping that I finally took action. And boy, am I glad I did!

Believe it or not, just one week after landscaping the property, we received an offer and the house was sold! It was a valuable lesson learned: Investing in the exterior of a property can make all the difference in attracting potential buyers and ultimately sealing the deal.

Landscaping has become a top priority for me, and I allocate a significant portion of my budget to it. I invest thousands of dollars in high-quality sod and ornamental plants to create a stunning exterior that complements my renovated homes. I'm hands-on in the process too—I visit the nursery with my landscaper, carefully selecting each plant and directing exactly where they should be placed. If you're new to fixing-and-flipping, you can always work with a landscape architect or a similar professional to effectively up your curb appeal.

Broker Breakdown: Researching, Auditioning, and Selecting the Best

When it comes to selling your renovated property, partnering with the right real estate broker can make all the difference. You need a knowledgeable and experienced agent who intimately understands the local market and can effectively showcase your property to potential buyers.

Research and Identify Top Brokers

When venturing into unfamiliar neighborhoods for projects, I employ a strategic approach to find the best broker. Here's how:

- **Research similar properties:** I start by researching similar properties in the area, taking note of the listing brokers and their sales records
- **Identify top-performing brokers:** I identify the top-performing brokers in the area, looking for those with a proven track record of success in the local market

The Broker Audition Process

Once I've identified potential brokers, I invite them to present a comprehensive listing strategy. This is essentially an audition, where I gauge their:

- **Expertise:** I assess their knowledge of the local market, including current trends, prices, and buyer demand
- **Marketing strategy:** I review their marketing plan, including how they intend to showcase my property to potential buyers
- **Communication style:** I evaluate their communication style, ensuring they're responsive, professional, and able to effectively represent my interests

Selecting the Best Broker

After the audition process, I select the broker who best meets my needs. This approach ensures I partner with a broker who:

- **Understands the local market:** Has intimate knowledge of the local market, including current trends and buyer demand
- **Can effectively showcase my property:** Has a solid marketing strategy in place to showcase my property to potential buyers
- **Aligns with my goals:** Shares my vision and goals for the project, ensuring we're working together toward a successful outcome

Developing a Marketing Strategy to Sell Your Flip Fast

To successfully sell your renovated property, it's essential to develop a tailored marketing plan, price it competitively, and prepare it for showings. Here's how to get the most bang for your buck.

Develop a Marketing Strategy

Craft a customized plan to showcase the property's unique features, targeting potential buyers through various channels. You'll want to determine when the property will be available for showings and make sure it is available on all real estate platforms (MLS, Zillow, Realtor.com, etc.). You can work with your broker to determine the key selling points of the property and include that in the listing description. The key to determining your marketing strategy is identifying your target buyer and thinking of where/how they will see your property. Key marketing elements include:

- **Sign riders:** Eye-catching signs highlighting the property's best features
- **Photo and virtual tours:** Immersive online experiences allowing buyers to explore the property remotely
- **Drone shots:** Aerial footage showcasing the property's exterior and surrounding area

The Power of Transparency in Your Flip

In addition to making sure I have a marketing strategy that will get the property in front of my target buyer, I always conduct pre-inspections on my properties to identify and address potential issues before buyers do. You can include the inspection report in your additional documentation with the listing information. This gives you the opportunity to know what an inspector flags ahead of the under-contract period of the sale. With the inspection report, you can either address the issues found or have some areas of negotiation with your buyer.

This proactive approach:

- **Builds trust:** Demonstrates transparency and accountability
- **Streamlines the sales process:** Allows buyers to make more informed offers, potentially eliminating the need for inspections

With fix-and-flip pre-inspections, you should hopefully have few things to address on the list from the inspector. It is important to use good contractors who can be proactive and complete the renovation the right way (under code and without cutting corners). However, there are some issues that can arise with a pre-inspection. If the property is inspected, you must disclose this information to the buyer. With the information in the buyer's hands, you might be in a situation where buyers negotiate a lower purchase price due to the number of issues that come up. They also might ask that you address the issues, or they will cancel the contract. This could cause problems for the deal (a property that goes in and out of contract can be a red flag for potential buyers).

I always err on the side of transparency, so even if something comes up in the inspection report, I'd rather the buyer know about it than purchase the property and be surprised (and potentially disappointed) later.

Competitive Pricing Strategies for Your Flip

Set a price that reflects the property's value, considering recent sales of comparable properties in the area. You can work with your real estate broker to determine what properties have sold for in the area your property is in, in addition to identifying properties that have similar upgrades and finishes to your property. This will help you determine how to price your property (and the justification behind the price, should a buyer submit an offer under asking price). Pricing your property accurately and competitively ensures:

- **Attracting serious buyers:** A competitive price attracts genuine buyers and encourages offers

- **Minimizing days on market:** A well-priced property sells faster, reducing holding costs

Prepare for Showings

Ensure the property is clean, well maintained, and ready for showings. This includes:

- **Cleaning and decluttering:** Presenting a tidy and organized space
- **Minor touch-ups:** Addressing any cosmetic issues to create a lasting impression

After years of flipping and selling homes, I've gained valuable insights into the importance of attention to detail in the final stages of a project. When I first started, I focused primarily on the renovations themselves, neglecting the critical aspects that come after. However, I quickly learned that these finishing touches are just as crucial as the renovations in securing a successful sale. By prioritizing these details, I've been able to maximize my returns, attract more buyers, and build a reputation for delivering high-quality properties.

From Concept to Cash: Real-Life Examples of Successful Flips

I want to share two personal case studies that illustrate the highs and lows of this business. Both projects involved full-gut renovations, but one yielded a substantial profit, while the other resulted in significant losses.

Fix-and-flip investing can be an exhilarating experience when profit margins are high and a substantial payday is on the horizon. However, the reality is far less glamorous when faced with significant losses. The emotional challenge of pouring time, effort, and resources into a property that's unlikely to yield a return can be daunting. Despite the financial disappointment, it's essential to maintain a professional mindset and continue to showcase the property in its best possible light, ensuring a smooth and efficient sale.

Example 1: This house had a unique character, with historic charm, a quirky floor plan, and an unfinished basement—exactly the kind of house that I like to renovate. This house required a top-to-bottom renovation: a new roof, siding, retaining walls, seismic retrofitting, basement waterproofing, and French drains. We also made dramatic changes to the interior, removing a century-old brick fireplace to open up the floor plan as well as taking down the main floor ceiling to reveal a stunning vaulted ceiling.

We ultimately transformed this property from a cozy two-bedroom, one-bathroom home into a spacious four-bedroom, three-bathroom residence, more than doubling its original capacity. We kept the exterior charm but made the inside modern, with beautiful quartz countertops, designer tile, and a thoughtful floor plan tailored for family living.

Project financials

- Purchase price: $720,000
- Rehab costs: $180,000
- Holding time: Nine months
- Holding costs: $70,000
- Buying/selling costs: $110,000
- Sales price: $1,240,000
- Total profit: $160,000

I loved this deal because the transformation was night and day. By thoroughly renovating every aspect of the house, I was able to create a completely new and stunning product that far exceeded its original form.

I strongly advise that only seasoned investors take on a project of this magnitude. Certain aspects required expertise that would be challenging for new investors to navigate. To mitigate risk, it's essential to choose projects that align with your experience and capabilities, as overestimating your abilities can lead to costly consequences—which brings me to my worst deal!

Example 2: I acquired this property in Raleigh, North Carolina. You may wonder why I took on this out-of-state challenge so far from my home. The reason is personal: My younger brother, an aspiring real estate investor, wanted to learn the ropes of house flipping. I saw this as an opportunity to mentor him remotely, with him serving as my boots on the ground. Given my experience with numerous projects, I was confident I could guide him through the process via phone, video calls, and other digital tools.

We acquired a stunning 3,500-square-foot home in Cary, North Carolia, nestled in a quiet cul-de-sac. The property boasted excellent curb appeal but required a full-gut renovation. To ensure we found the right contractor for the job, I flew to Raleigh and, together with my brother, interviewed seven or eight potential contractors.

After carefully evaluating each candidate's pros and cons, we selected the most experienced contractor. We took the extra step of visiting one of his recently flipped homes in the area and verifying his references. Confident in his abilities, we moved forward with the renovation project.

The first major issue arose three months into the project. Our contractor suddenly stopped showing up to the jobsite. We were shocked and concerned, as he was responsible for pulling all necessary permits. As we investigated further, we discovered that not only had he failed to obtain the permits but he had also ripped out parts of the house that were not supposed to be touched.

Despite repeated attempts to communicate with the contractor and his team, we were met with silence. It became clear that we had to cut our losses and move on. Unfortunately, this decision came at a significant cost: We were already over budget and behind schedule.

Our struggles with contractors didn't end there. We had two more failed attempts with different contractors before finally finding one who was ethical, trustworthy, and competent. The renovation, which should have taken six to seven months to complete, ultimately took thirteen months. The experience was frustrating and costly, but it taught us valuable lessons.

My brother proved to be an absolute rock star throughout this challenging project. Despite the numerous setbacks, he demonstrated remarkable resilience, showing up every day with a positive attitude and unwavering dedication. His exceptional work ethic was inspiring, as he tackled each issue head-on and continued to push the project forward.

From across the country, I did my best to provide support and guidance, but my brother's boots-on-the-ground efforts were instrumental in keeping the project moving. His commitment and perseverance played a huge role in ultimately bringing this renovation to fruition.

After completing the renovation, we listed the property for sale, but yet another hurdle emerged. Despite being confident in the quality of the work, the lack of permits initially obtained by the previous contractor proved to be a major turnoff for potential buyers. Even though the construction was done to code, buyers were hesitant to take on the risk.

The property lingered on the market for six months, and we realized we needed to take action. We decided to pull "already built construction" permits, which allowed us to obtain necessary permits even after completion. This process required us to open up some walls for inspection of the framing, electrical, and plumbing, but it ultimately gave us the certification we needed.

With the permits in hand, we finally attracted a buyer and closed on the property. It was a long and arduous journey, but the sense of relief and accomplishment was well worth it.

Our initial projections promised a hefty profit of $300,000 when we first acquired the property. However, the reality was starkly different. The prolonged timelines, budget overruns, and unforeseen setbacks ultimately led to a devastating outcome: We incurred a substantial loss.

Project financials
- **Purchase price:** $495,000
- **Rehab costs:** $250,000
- **Holding time:** Eighteen months
- **Holding costs:** $140,000
- **Buying/selling costs:** $100,000
- **Sales price:** $850,000
- **Total loss:** $135,000

Here are some lessons learned from this deal.

- When venturing out of state, I learned it's wise to start small. A cosmetic rehab would've been a better initial approach rather than diving into a full-gut renovation.
- **Thoroughly vet contractors:** The initial contractor's failure to obtain permits and abandoning the project led to significant delays and costs
- **Regularly monitor progress:** Keeping a close eye on the project's progress could have helped identify issues earlier, mitigating some of the damage
- **Budget for contingencies and holding costs:** Unexpected expenses and delays can quickly add up. Having a contingency fund in place can help absorb these shocks. Holding costs, such as financing and property maintenance, can quickly add up. Factoring these costs into the initial budget is essential.
- **Be prepared for the unexpected:** Renovation projects often come with surprises. Staying flexible and adapting to changing circumstances is crucial for success.

As I reflect on my journey in fix-and-flip investing, I'm reminded of the countless lessons learned, the triumphs, and the setbacks. This business has tested my resolve, pushed me to grow, and taught me the value of perseverance. But most importantly, it's given me the opportunity to transform lives, one house at a time.

There's something profoundly satisfying about taking a neglected property and breathing new life into it. Seeing the before and after, witnessing the joy on a buyer's face when they find their dream home—it's a feeling that never gets old.

If you're considering embarking on this journey, I want to leave you with a message of encouragement.

Learning to flip homes successfully equips you with a versatile tool kit for assessing real estate opportunities. By mastering the art of flipping houses, you'll gain a unique perspective on building equity—one that can't be replicated in many other forms of investing. Selling your property is just as crucial as the renovation process itself. By understanding the local market, pricing your property correctly, and leveraging creative marketing strategies, you can maximize your returns and achieve a profitable exit.

Whether you choose to work with a real estate agent, sell directly to an investor, or explore alternative sales methods, the key is to be flexible, adaptable, and open to innovative approaches. By thinking outside the box and staying focused on your goals, you can turn your fix-and-flip project into a resounding success, setting yourself up for long-term success in the world of real estate investing.

Let's look at the specific lessons you should take away from this chapter.

NEW-TO-THE-GAME NOAH

Begin with simple flips that involve cosmetic upgrades like:

- Painting.
- Landscaping.

These easy-to-navigate projects are perfect for:

- Assembling your dream team.
- Learning from others' experiences.
- Building confidence for future deals.

Level up your skills, and get ready to crush your fix-and-flip goals!

ACTIVE ALEX

With your extensive hands-on experience, it's time to optimize your fix-and-flip strategy.

Optimize

- Leverage your network to access top-tier deals
- Map out efficient project workflows
- Continuously refine your systems to boost speed and precision
- Focus on high-return renovations, prioritizing upgrades with the greatest impact
- Develop a robust risk management plan to navigate unexpected setbacks

Expand

- Explore opportunities for scaling, such as partnering with investors or expanding your team
- Stay up to date with market trends, adapting your strategy to remain competitive

Diversify
- Diversify your portfolio by exploring other investment strategies, such as rental properties or wholesaling
- Build a strong online presence to attract potential buyers, investors, and partners
- Continuously educate yourself through workshops, webinars, and industry events

By implementing these strategies, you'll be well equipped to take your fix-and-flip business to the next level and achieve long-term success.

PIVOT PEYTON

Consider harnessing the potential of fix-and-flips to redefine your real estate journey. This strategy can be a catalyst for growth, allowing you to:

- Leverage existing skills and expertise.
- Experiment with innovative ideas and property types.
- Refine your craft with each new project.
- Continuously expand and diversify your portfolio.

Embracing fix-and-flips can be a thrilling way to pivot and reignite your passion for real estate. By combining familiarity with exploration, you'll be poised for exciting new opportunities and long-term success.

SEASONED-INVESTOR SAM

As a seasoned veteran, you're poised to take your real estate empire to new heights. Here's my advice.

- Don't plateau: Continuously challenge yourself with high-reward flips that showcase your expertise
- Tackle complexity: Take on intricate projects that push your skills and refine your strategies
- Scale up: Leverage profits to fuel bigger, more ambitious deals and endeavors

- Think beyond fix-and-flip: View each project as a stepping stone toward achieving your broader goals of wealth and success

As a seasoned investor, you have the experience and expertise to:

- Explore new markets and asset classes.
- Develop strategic partnerships and collaborations.
- Build a robust real estate portfolio.
- Create a lasting legacy in the industry.

Remember, your journey is far from over. Keep pushing boundaries, innovating, and striving for excellence. The sky's the limit!

LONG-GAME LOGAN

As a visionary investor, you're building a lasting real estate legacy. Here's how fix-and-flip can play a strategic role.

- Use short-term flip profits to fuel long-term investments aligned with your ultimate vision
- Focus on neighborhoods poised for growth, where flips can generate strong returns and create a foundation for future success
- Prioritize properties with potential for appreciation, rental income, or both
- Continuously monitor market trends and adjust your strategy to stay ahead of the curve

By integrating fix-and-flip into your long-game strategy, you'll:

- Accelerate wealth creation.
- Diversify your portfolio.
- Build a strong foundation for future generations.
- Leave a lasting impact on the real estate landscape.

Remember, every successful flip is a chapter in your ongoing legacy. Write it wisely!

Chapter 11

Exit Strategies—Selling Your Property with Ease

A few years ago, I bought a house in Tacoma, Washington, with the intention of flipping it. At the time, I wasn't very familiar with the area, but I trusted the wholesaler I bought it from—someone I had worked with before and who took the time to walk me through the details of the property. He explained that Tacoma was experiencing a significant housing shortage, with high demand for both rentals and SFHs.

Typically, I focus on full-gut renovations: projects that require taking a property down to the studs. But this house was different. It didn't need a major overhaul, which made it a bit of an outlier for me. Given its condition and the strong rental demand in the area, I made the strategic decision to hold it as a rental rather than flip it right away.

My plan was to keep it for at least two years to avoid short-term capital gains taxes. When that period was up, I made some light upgrades: fresh paint, new flooring, and updated appliances. Then I listed it for sale and ended up selling it for double what I had paid.

That experience was a game changer. It showed me the value of strategic timing and minimal renovation—and opened my eyes to the potential of low-effort, high-reward property sales.

There are countless paths to success in real estate. In the last chapter, we explored one of the most popular strategies: the fix-and-flip. But that's just one of many opportunities available to you.

Selling Your Property as a Low-Effort Exit Strategy

As you evaluate your property's performance, regardless of the strategy you're using (short-, medium-, or long-term renting), you may find that selling the property would be the most profitable for you. This profit could be something other than financial; you may want to release yourself from being a landlord or get rid of an STR that you're no longer using as your own vacation property. The reasons why you might sell a property are endless. But what should you do before you sell the property?

The sweat equity and fix-and-flip strategies demonstrate how adding value to a property can, well, add value to the property. Both involve lots of time and work to renovate the property and prepare it for sale. There is another approach that requires less effort and resources. Instead of a lengthy renovation timeline and all the energy it takes to get one to the finish line, you can sell your property without making significant updates or changes. This strategy is often referred to as a "low-effort exit" or "as-is sale." Like any opportunity, there are pros and cons.

Benefits of Selling Your Property in Its Current State

- **Minimized renovation costs:** By not investing in renovations, you can save thousands of dollars in construction costs, permits, and labor expenses
- **Faster sale:** Selling a property as is can speed up the sale process, because you're not waiting for renovations to be completed
- **Less stress:** With fewer responsibilities and deadlines to manage, selling a property as is can be a more relaxed experience
- **Potential for quick cash:** If you're in a situation where you need to access cash quickly, selling a property as is can provide a rapid influx of funds

Challenges of Selling Your Property As Is

- **Lower sales price:** Buyers may be deterred by a property's outdated or damaged condition, leading to lower offers or a longer sale period
- **Limited buyer pool:** Some buyers may be hesitant to purchase a property that needs significant repairs or updates, reducing the pool of potential buyers
- **Inspection and due diligence issues:** Buyers may uncover hidden problems during inspections, which can lead to renegotiations or even canceled sales
- **Potential losses:** If you're unable to sell the property quickly or for a reasonable price, you may end up losing money on the investment

Mitigating Potential Pitfalls When Selling Your Property

Don't let that list of challenges scare you away. Yes, it is important to be realistic, but that doesn't mean that you need to lean into the doom and gloom of the situation either. To minimize potential losses when selling a property as is, there are several ways you can mitigate and offset the downsides of this style of investment.

- **Price the property competitively:** Research the market to determine a fair and competitive price for the property in its current condition. You can use the BiggerPockets Market Finder to help with this research (www.BiggerPockets.com/BookMarkets).
- **Disclose known issues:** Be transparent about the property's condition and any known problems to avoid potential disputes with buyers
- **Highlight the property's potential:** Emphasize the property's positive features and potential for renovation or redevelopment to attract buyers looking for a fixer-upper
- **Be prepared to negotiate:** Be flexible and open to negotiations, as buyers may try to lowball their offers or request repairs

You can learn more about negotiation tactics in *The Book on Negotiating Real Estate* by J Scott, Carol Scott, and Mark Ferguson. www.BiggerPockets.com/ReadNegotiating

In the past, I've sold homes as is for one of two reasons: either I had maximized the equity in the deal—meaning the property's value had appreciated significantly over time, but the rental income hadn't kept pace, limiting further returns—or I had identified a more lucrative opportunity that required immediate capital.

"Maximizing equity," in this context, refers to reaching a point where the property's market value has grown substantially, but the income it generates (like rent) remains relatively flat. Holding the asset longer may still yield gains, but the bulk of the value has already been captured, and the opportunity cost of not reallocating that equity becomes too high.

Here are ten scenarios where selling a property might be the best exit strategy.

1. **Too difficult to manage:** If you're finding it challenging to manage the property due to issues like problem tenants, frequent repairs, or difficult neighbors, selling might be the best option

2. **Too many properties:** If you've accumulated multiple properties and are struggling to manage them all, selling the least profitable or most problematic ones can help streamline your portfolio

3. **Change in market conditions:** If the local market has shifted, making it less favorable for rentals or renovations, selling might be a good idea. This could be due to changes in local zoning laws, a decline in property values, or an increase in competition.

4. **Personal or financial circumstances:** If your personal or financial situation has changed, making it difficult to continue investing in real estate, selling a property might be necessary. This could be due to a job loss, health issues, or a need for liquidity.

5. **Lack of cash flow:** If a property is consistently generating negative cash flow or not meeting your expected returns, selling might be a good option

6. **End of the investment cycle:** If you've reached the end of your intended investment cycle, selling a property can help you realize your profits and redeploy your capital into new investments

7. **Partner or investor exit:** If you have partners or investors in a property and they want to exit the investment, selling the property might be the best option

8. **Property condition:** If a property has significant maintenance or repair issues that are too costly to address, selling as is might be a good option

9. **Tax implications:** If selling a property can help you minimize tax liabilities or maximize tax benefits, it might be a good exit strategy

Talk to your CPA or tax planner to come up with your cost basis for each property you are planning to sell, so you understand the tax implications of that sale.

10. **Reinvestment opportunities:** If you've identified more attractive investment opportunities that align with your goals and risk tolerance, selling a property can provide the necessary funds to pursue those opportunities

What Types of Properties Are Suitable for a Quick Sale?

In addition to looking at your personal levels of experience and preferences, it is also a good idea to look at the kind of property you are dealing with. When making a decision on this strategy, both are equally important pieces of the equation. Properties that are good candidates for a quick sale include:

- **Properties that require a lipstick or cosmetic makeover:** Properties that are in great condition but just need a quick paint, carpet, and appliance update
- **Inherited or estate properties:** Properties inherited or acquired through estate sales might be sold as is to simplify the transfer process and avoid costly renovations
- **Properties with high maintenance costs:** Properties with high maintenance costs, such as older homes or those with outdated systems, might be sold as is to avoid ongoing expenses
- **Properties in declining neighborhoods:** Properties located in neighborhoods with declining property values or increasing crime rates might be sold as is to minimize losses
- **Properties with environmental or structural issues:** Properties with environmental hazards, such as lead paint or asbestos, or structural issues, like foundation problems, might be sold as is to avoid costly remediation

Most people think there's only one way to sell a property: List it, find a buyer, hand over the keys, and cash the check. But that's a narrow view. Selling isn't just the end of a deal; it's a strategic move that can shape your entire investing future.

You've probably heard the saying, "You make your money when you buy." And while there's truth to that, I'd argue the real wealth-building happens in how you exit.

A smart, well-timed sale can unlock equity, minimize taxes, and fuel your next big move. It's not just about letting go of a property; it's about setting yourself up for what's next.

Seller Financing: Unconventional Wisdom for a Creative Exit

One of the most powerful—and often overlooked—exit strategies is becoming the bank for your buyer.

I'll never forget the first time I used seller financing to exit a deal. I had a property that had appreciated nicely, but I wasn't in a rush to sell it off the traditional way. I wanted to maximize my return, keep some cash flow coming in, and maybe—just maybe—structure something a little more creative.

That's when I leaned into seller financing.

Instead of having the buyer go through a bank and deal with endless paperwork and lender delays, I became the bank. I offered to finance part of the purchase price myself. The buyer was thrilled—they got to bypass the traditional mortgage route, and I got to set the terms: interest rate, monthly payments, timeline. It was a win-win.

Not only did I sell the property at a premium, but I also created a new stream of monthly income—*on my terms*. No appraisals, no underwriters, no middleman. Just a direct agreement between two people trying to make a deal work.

What I realized then was this: Seller financing isn't just a workaround; it's a smart, strategic play. It opens the door to more buyers, gives you control over the deal, and can turn a one-time sale into a long-term income stream.

The Benefits of Seller Financing
- **Increased buyer pool:** By offering seller financing, you can attract buyers who may not qualify for traditional financing or who prefer the flexibility of a private financing arrangement. Examples can include buyers with past credit

issues, individuals with high debt-to-income ratios, and entrepreneurs with variable income.

- **Negotiating power:** As the financier, you have more negotiating power to set the terms of the sale, including the price, interest rate, and payment schedule
- **Potential for higher returns:** Seller financing can provide a higher ROI than traditional sales, as you earn interest on the loan amount
- **Tax benefits:** Seller financing can provide tax benefits, such as spreading out capital gains tax over the life of the loan
- **Ongoing income:** Since the buyer is essentially getting their mortgage from you, they'll pay you monthly installments for the life of that loan—which can be years or even decades

The Challenges of Seller Financing

When considering seller financing, keep in mind the potential risks and considerations. One major concern is that the buyer may default on the loan, forcing you to take back the property and potentially sell it again. Additionally, you'll need to ensure compliance with local and federal regulations, such as usury laws and disclosure requirements. If you pursue this path, I would highly recommend that you hire an attorney to draw up all the documents. It's also crucial to conduct thorough due diligence on the buyer to verify their creditworthiness and ability to make payments, helping to minimize the risk of default.

The bottom line is that the risk is sometimes worth taking because by considering seller financing as an exit strategy, you can differentiate yourself from other sellers, attract more buyers, and potentially earn a higher return on your investment.

Types of Seller Financing: Exploring Your Options

- **Owner financing:** You, the seller, finance the entire purchase price of the property
- **Wraparound mortgage:** If you have an existing mortgage, then you, the seller, can wrap a new mortgage around the existing mortgage, allowing the buyer to make payments to you

A wraparound mortgage is a type of financing where a seller extends credit to a buyer by essentially becoming the lender themselves, while the existing mortgage on the property remains in place and is not paid off. The buyer makes payments to the seller, who then uses those funds to pay off the existing mortgage and pockets the difference, often in the form of a higher interest rate.

- **Lease option:** You, the seller, lease the property to the buyer with an option to purchase, often with a portion of the rent applied to the down payment

One of the most crucial parts of selling your property? Finding the right buyer. As I like to say, *No buyer, no bueno.* It might sound simple, but the truth is, not all buyers are created equal—and the type of buyer you attract can make or break your deal.

So how do you find that perfect match? The key to finding your buyer will depend on marketing your property effectively so that it speaks directly to the kind of buyer you want to attract.

Meet Your Buyer: Who's Purchasing Your Property?

When selling a property, you'll typically encounter two types of buyers: investors and homeowners.

- **Investors:** Investors are looking for properties that can generate rental income, appreciate in value, or be renovated for resale. They often prioritize properties with potential for high returns, cash flow, and tax benefits.
- **Homeowners:** Homeowners, on the other hand, are looking for a primary residence or a vacation home. They prioritize properties that meet their needs, lifestyle, and budget.

Tailoring Your Marketing Approach for Investors vs. Homeowners

To effectively market your property, you'll need to tailor your approach to the type of buyer you're targeting. Makes sense, right? Different property uses results in different needs and desires. Be sure to keep this in mind when telling the world (or at least, the local market) about the property you have to offer.

Marketing to Those Looking for a Deal

To attract investors, focus on highlighting these aspects about the property:

- Rental income potential
- Cash flow projections
- Appreciation potential
- Tax benefits
- Renovation or redevelopment opportunities

When broadcasting this information, I recommend that you use online platforms, such as LoopNet, Zillow, or Redfin to reach a wider audience of investors. Also, be aware that investors love buying deals off-market, so use Facebook or Neighborhood groups to market.

Marketing to Families and Individuals

To attract homeowners, focus on highlighting these aspects about the property:

- Best features and amenities
- Location and neighborhood
- Condition and upgrades
- Potential for customization or renovation

When communicating to homeowners, I recommend you use social media, online real estate platforms, and local advertising to reach a wider audience of homeowners.

While you can market and sell your property independently, using a real estate agent can be beneficial. If you are short on time, agents can handle marketing, showings, and negotiations, freeing up your time. If you are unfamiliar with the local market, agents who have extensive knowledge of the local market, pricing, and buyer preferences can assist you in making those crucial decisions. Finally, if you want to maximize your sales price, a real estate agent can help you price your property competitively and negotiate with buyers to get the best possible sales price. Remember, though, that using an agent will typically involve paying a commission fee of 4–6 percent of the sales price.

Strategic Exit Strategies for Multiple Properties

Selling multiple properties at once, known as a "portfolio deal," can be a great way to streamline your investments and maximize returns. This strategy allows you to simplify your portfolio, reducing management responsibilities and overhead costs.

By selling multiple properties together, you can attract higher offers from buyers who are willing to pay a premium for the convenience of acquiring multiple properties at once. This can be a win-win for both you and the buyer. Additionally, you can use the proceeds from a portfolio sale to diversify your investments and explore new opportunities.

One of the benefits of doing a portfolio deal is the efficiency. You'll only need to go through the sales process once rather than multiple times. This can save you time and effort. Portfolio deals can also attract institutional buyers, private equity firms, and other investors looking for bulk acquisitions.

However, portfolio deals can be complex and involve multiple properties, which can add complexity to the transaction. You'll need to carefully price each property and ensure that the buyer is qualified and capable of completing the purchase. Despite these challenges, portfolio deals can be a great way to exit your investments and achieve your goals.

Costs to Consider When Selling Your Property

Like any real estate deal, it's good to know what you are getting into ahead of time. Portfolio sales are no different. When selling your property, it's essential to factor in the various costs involved.

Here are some key expenses to consider.

- **Real estate agent commission:** Typically 4–6 percent of the sales price, this is the fee paid to the agent for their services
- **Closing costs:** These costs, usually 1–3 percent of the sales price, cover fees associated with transferring ownership, such as title insurance, escrow fees, and recording fees
- **Repairs and renovations:** You may need to invest in repairs or renovations to make your property more attractive to buyers
- **Staging and decorating:** Hiring a professional stager or decorator can help showcase your property's potential, but this comes at a cost
- **Inspections and appraisals:** You may need to pay for inspections or appraisals to identify potential issues or determine the property's value
- **Taxes and fees:** Consider any outstanding taxes, liens, or fees associated with the property. This includes real estate transfer tax in most states.
- **Marketing and advertising:** You may need to pay for marketing and advertising efforts to attract potential buyers, like investing in high-quality photos, social media campaigns, and virtual video tours
- **Attorney fees:** Depending on the complexity of the sale, you may need to hire an attorney to review contracts and negotiate on your behalf

By factoring in these costs, you can better prepare yourself for the financial aspects of selling your property.

By considering the benefits and drawbacks of each exit strategy, you can make informed decisions that align with your investment objectives. Remember to stay flexible, adapt to changing market conditions, and continually evaluate your exit options to ensure the best possible outcome.

Investors Who Can Profit from the "Selling Your Property" Strategy

Who is this strategy a good match for? Here are four types of investors who could benefit most from as-is selling.

1. **Rookies:** This strategy can be a good fit for rookie investors who are new to real estate investing. It provides a relatively easy entry and exit point, allowing them to gain experience and build confidence without taking on excessive risk.
2. **Busy professionals:** Investors with limited time or those who are busy with other commitments may find this strategy appealing. It requires less time and effort compared to other strategies, such as fix-and-flip or rental property management.
3. **Risk-averse investors:** Those who are risk averse or prefer a more conservative approach to real estate investing may prefer the "selling your property" strategy. It allows them to exit the investment quickly, minimizing their exposure to market fluctuations and other risks.
4. **Investors with limited capital:** Investors with limited capital may find this strategy attractive, as it requires less up-front capital compared to other strategies

A note for experienced and advanced investors—while this strategy can benefit experienced investors, you may find it less appealing due to its relatively lower potential returns. Intermediate investors might consider this strategy to exit a property that's not performing well quickly or free up capital for more lucrative investments. Advanced investors might use this strategy to rebalance their portfolios or take advantage of tax benefits.

Let's look at how this applies to our characters. Hopefully these audience-focused action steps help you make forward progress on your own real estate journey!

NEW-TO-THE-GAME NOAH

Before diving into the as-is sale strategy, take some time to do your homework. Here's a suggested learning plan.

- Get familiar with local market comps: Research how as-is sales are performing in your area to understand the potential demand and pricing
- Study successful case studies: Look into properties sold using the as-is strategy to gain insight into the process and identify potential pitfalls

- Learn from experienced investors: Attend a real estate meetup or webinar to connect with seasoned investors and gain a deeper understanding of low-effort exit strategies

By educating yourself, you'll be better equipped to decide if the as-is sale strategy aligns with your investment goals and approach.

ACTIVE ALEX

Consider optimizing your portfolio by off-loading an underperforming or high-maintenance property. Here's a step-by-step plan.

1. Portfolio audit: Evaluate your current holdings to identify a property that's dragging down your returns or consuming excessive resources
2. Research investor-friendly platforms: Look into listing platforms that cater to investors, such as Hubzu or Xome. These platforms can help you reach a targeted audience of potential buyers.
3. Market effectively: Showcase your property's potential by highlighting its best features and providing detailed documentation, including property reports and inspection records
4. Free up resources: By selling off an underperforming property, you'll liberate time and capital to focus on more promising opportunities, ultimately strengthening your portfolio and accelerating your growth

By streamlining your portfolio, you'll be able to concentrate on higher-yielding investments and continue to build your real estate empire.

PIVOT PEYTON

As a strategic and adaptable investor, you may find seller financing to be a game-changing approach. By exploring this option, you can:

- Maximize profits through interest payments.
- Maintain cash flow through regular installments.
- Attract buyers who may not qualify for traditional financing.

To ensure a smooth transition into seller financing, consider consulting with a real estate attorney. They will help you:

- Navigate the legalities and regulations surrounding seller financing.
- Structure a deal that protects your interests and addresses all necessary terms.
- Confidently move forward, knowing you've covered all the bases.

By embracing seller financing, you can expand your investment tool kit and unlock new opportunities for growth and profitability.

SEASONED-INVESTOR SAM

As a seasoned investor, you're likely evaluating your portfolio on a continuous basis to optimize returns. Consider the following strategy.

- Portfolio rebalancing: Assess your current holdings to determine if selling a property as is could help rebalance your portfolio, freeing up capital for more promising opportunities
- Alternative exit strategies: Evaluate whether structuring a wraparound mortgage or lease option could maximize returns on a specific property. These strategies can provide a steady income stream while minimizing up-front costs.

By exploring these options, you can refine your investment approach, optimize your portfolio, and continue to drive growth and profitability.

LONG-GAME LOGAN

Take a moment to assess your long-term investment strategy. Ask yourself:

- Could an as-is sale or seller financing accelerate your progress toward your goals?
- Are there properties in your portfolio that no longer align with your vision?

- Are there better opportunities to reinvest your capital and drive future growth?

Don't get caught up in the idea that playing the long game means every decision needs to take forever. Identify areas for improvement, research new opportunities, and take decisive action.

Remember, leveraging strategies like as-is sales or seller financing can help you:

- Optimize your portfolio for long-term success.
- Reinvest capital into higher-growth opportunities.
- Stay focused on your goals while adapting to changing market conditions.

Keep playing the long game, but don't be afraid to make strategic moves that drive progress.

Chapter 12

Swap and Grow Rich— Mastering the 1031 Exchange

As a savvy investor or business owner, you've worked tirelessly to build wealth through real estate or other investment assets. But when it's time to exit, taxes can take a significant bite out of your hard-earned profits. That's where the strategic power of 1031 exchanges come into play. Because once you do all that buying and selling, you'd like to keep as much of that profit as possible, right? The good news is that you can, using this special strategy.

A 1031 exchange, also known as a like-kind exchange, is a tax-deferred strategy that allows you to swap one investment property for another, potentially saving hundreds of thousands of dollars in capital gains taxes.

First, you sell your property. Then, within a prescribed amount of time, you use the money from that sale to buy another property. As long as both properties meet qualifications and both transactions happen within the allowed amount of time, you won't have an immediate tax burden on the sale income from the first property.

More specifically, this exchange gives you the following tax benefits:

- **Defers capital gains tax:** Delay paying taxes on profits from the sale of the original property
- **Defers depreciation recapture tax:** Delay paying taxes on previously claimed depreciation deductions
- **Preserves tax basis:** Transfer the original property's tax basis to the new property, potentially reducing future taxes

This creative real estate exit strategy can be a huge help for investors seeking to rebalance their portfolios, diversify their assets, or simply unlock liquidity without triggering a taxable event. It allows you to reinvest the full proceeds from your sale while diversifying your portfolio.

Whether you're a seasoned pro or just starting out, this chapter will give you the lowdown on tax-deferred exchanges and how to make them work for you.

Remember, it's essential to consult with a tax professional or attorney to ensure compliance with all rules and regulations, as always.

What Qualifies for a 1031 Exchange?

Next, let's look at what kind of properties might be eligible for this specific kind of tax break.

- **Investment properties:** Rental properties, commercial buildings, and other income-generating properties
- **Real estate:** Land, buildings, and other real estate assets
- **Like-kind properties:** Properties of the same nature or character (e.g., exchanging one rental property for another)

You will note that there's nothing on this list about the properties being the same type of building or having similar values. You can absolutely exchange an SFH for a fourplex, for example—as you'll see below, that's what I did for my very first 1031.

But not every type of property is eligible for this kind of exchange. You can't do a 1031 exchange for certain types of properties and assets.

- **Primary residences:** Personal homes or residences
- **Second homes:** Vacation homes or other personal residences
- **Personal property:** Assets like art, collectibles, or other personal items

That's not as limiting as it might sound. In fact, it means the 1031 exchange is perfect for real estate investors like us, who don't live in the properties we invest in and who want to diversify, upgrade, or otherwise optimize our portfolios.

A Step-by-Step Guide to Completing a 1031 Exchange

As always, I want to be as helpful as possible. So here is a rundown on the steps you need to take when working through the 1031 exchange process. If you get stuck or need help, check out this BiggerPockets resource: www.BiggerPockets.com/BookBlog1031Exchange.

1. **Identify a replacement property:** Find a new property to purchase within forty-five days of selling the original property. You don't have to have this new property lined up before the next step, but you do have only forty-five days from selling your property to identify it, so starting early is never a bad idea.
2. **Sell the original property:** Close the sale of the original property
3. **Use a qualified intermediary (QI):** Engage a QI to facilitate the exchange and hold the sale proceeds

A qualified intermediary (QI) is an independent third-party entity who facilitates a 1031 exchange by holding the sale proceeds and ensuring compliance with IRS regulations.

4. **Purchase the replacement property:** Close the purchase of the new property within 180 days of selling the original property.

Timing Is Everything: Rules and Deadlines to Keep in Mind

As far as strategies go, there are some pretty strict rules and regulations that surround this one. Stepping outside of these guidelines could result in losing the opportunities a 1031 can offer, so be very careful to follow them.

- **45-day rule:** Identify a replacement property within forty-five days of selling the original property
- **180-day rule:** Purchase the replacement property within 180 days of selling the original property
- **3-property rule:** Identify up to three replacement properties, regardless of value
- **95 percent rule:** Purchase at least 95 percent of the value of the identified replacement properties

When navigating a 1031 exchange, it's not just about identifying a like-kind property and racing the clock. To ensure a smooth and compliant transaction, there are several key details you'll want to address along the way.

Financing

If the full proceeds from the sale of your original property don't cover at least 95 percent of the cost of your replacement property, you'll need to secure additional financing. This can include traditional loans, private money, or creative financing options. Just make sure the debt on the new property is equal to or greater than the debt on the relinquished one—or you risk triggering taxes on the difference.

Title Issues

Title matters in a 1031 exchange are nonnegotiable. You must ensure clear title on both your relinquished and replacement properties. Any title issues—liens, encumbrances, or ownership discrepancies—can delay or derail the exchange entirely. It's worth doing a full title review and working with an experienced title company or attorney early in the process.

Entity Structure

Your entity structure matters more than you might think. The same taxpayer (or entity) that sells the original property must be the one to purchase the replacement. If your original property is held in an LLC, trust, or partnership, you'll want to ensure your replacement property is titled the same way. Shifting structures mid-exchange can lead to disqualification. This is where a CPA and real estate attorney can be invaluable allies.

What does this look like in real life? Twenty years ago, my husband and I took the plunge and bought our first home, a charming townhouse near Microsoft's Redmond campus. Fast-forward six years, and we upgraded to a new primary residence, turning our first home into our first investment property. It performed well, with great tenants and a doubling of its value. But as the equity grew, the rent didn't keep pace, so we started to think about selling it. That's when we stumbled upon 1031 exchanges. We were amazed—we could sell our underperforming property, upgrade to something bigger, and pay zero capital gains taxes? It sounded too good to be true!

We seized the opportunity, exchanging our cozy townhome for a fourplex in Seattle's vibrant Queen Anne neighborhood. The property was distressed, which meant, although it came with a lot of work, we snagged a great deal. With some TLC, I could renovate, boost rents, and instantly create additional equity. It was a win-win!

With $300,000 in equity from our townhome, we were able to purchase a new property with a down payment of $300,000 or less. This led us to a fantastic opportunity in the $1.2 million fourplex. By leveraging our existing equity, we were able to invest in a significantly more valuable property, amplifying our potential for long-term growth and returns.

Deal metrics				
	2020 value	Rent	2025 value	Rent
Townhome	$500,000	$2,100	$650,000	$2,800
Fourplex	$1,200,000	$4,000	$1,500,000	$8,200

As you can see, our strategic 1031 exchange yielded a substantial surge in both equity and rental income. This creative exit set us up for a lifetime of tax-deferred wealth growth.

After knocking it out of the park with my first 1031 exchange, I decided to do it all again. A few years ago, I subdivided a lot into three parcels and sold them off individually, scoring a sweet seven-figure profit. But instead of paying a hefty tax bill, I did another 1031 exchange.

This time around, I traded those parcels for a distressed office building in downtown Seattle—right in the heart of tech country, with giants like Meta, Amazon, and Apple on the same street. The building needed some love, but that made it affordable. I snapped it up, renovated it, and got it stabilized. Future plans for this building? You guessed it—I will 1031 exchange it into another distressed property. It could be a single-family house, multifamily, or another office building—the options are limitless. I cannot wait to do another one this year! This tax-saving strategy will allow us to continue scaling our investments and building a legacy of wealth that we can pass on to our kids tax free, which will create a lasting impact for generations to come.

Before we get to our characters, I'm going to say this again: It's absolutely essential to consult with a tax professional or attorney to ensure compliance with all rules and regulations. A 1031 only works if you are fully compliant with tax law, and tax law is not something you want to try to figure out yourself. Plus, this chapter is a general overview of the 1031 exchange, not a deep dive into all its ins and outs. Use this chapter as your starting point and then see an expert to help carry you the rest of the way.

NEW-TO-THE-GAME NOAH

Don't wait until you've already invested in a property to learn about 1031 exchanges. Start educating yourself now. Here's a step-by-step plan.

- Consult a tax pro: Schedule a meeting with a real estate–savvy CPA to discuss the benefits of 1031 exchanges and how they can fit into your long-term investment strategy
- Understand the rules: Familiarize yourself with the 45-day and 180-day deadlines for identifying and closing on a replacement property
- Consider your investment goals: Think about how 1031 exchanges can help you achieve your investment objectives, such as diversifying your portfolio or increasing cash flow

By getting a head start on learning about 1031 exchanges, you'll be better equipped to make informed decisions when opportunities arise. Remember, knowledge is power, and being prepared can help you avoid costly mistakes.

ACTIVE ALEX

As a hands-on investor, you'll love leveraging 1031 exchanges to grow your portfolio. By the time you trade up to a multifamily unit, you'll have built not just equity but experience. Here's a strategy tailored to your skills.

- Target distressed properties: Focus on finding properties that need renovation, where you can add value with your DIY skills
- Renovate and create equity: Improve the property, increase its value, and build significant equity

- Leverage equity into larger properties: Use the tax-deferred equity to acquire larger properties, like multifamily units, without paying taxes
- Start small, scale up: Begin with a smaller property, like a townhouse, and gradually move to larger projects
- Partner with a QI: Work with a professional to handle the 1031 exchange paperwork and logistics
- Plan renovations carefully: Stay on schedule, and use the tax deferral to boost your buying power for even bigger projects

By combining your DIY skills with strategic 1031 exchanges, you'll be unstoppable!

💡 PIVOT PEYTON

Your creative approach to investing makes you a natural fit for 1031 exchanges. Here's how to leverage your strengths.

- Stay ahead of market trends: Keep a pulse on the market to identify emerging opportunities, like the land subdivision example
- Spot adaptable properties: Focus on properties that offer room for creative experimentation and innovation
- Navigate rules and regulations: Your flexibility and adaptability will serve you well in navigating the strict rules surrounding 1031 exchanges
- Unleash your innovative strategies: Use your creativity to add value to properties and make them thrive

By combining your creative vision with the tax benefits of 1031 exchanges, you'll be able to:

- Stay agile in a changing market.
- Unlock hidden potential in properties.
- Build a diverse and resilient portfolio.

Keep pushing the boundaries of what's possible, Peyton!

SEASONED-INVESTOR SAM

As an experienced investor, you're well positioned to maximize the benefits of 1031 exchanges. Here's a strategy to consider.

- Scale up your portfolio: Use 1031 exchanges to trade multiple smaller properties for larger, more lucrative investments
- Target commercial or multifamily properties: Align your exchanges with your long-term goals, focusing on properties that offer substantial returns
- Collaborate with a tax professional: Fine-tune your strategy with expert guidance to ensure optimal tax benefits
- Leverage your network: Tap into your extensive network to uncover lucrative replacement properties within the forty-five-day window
- Focus on legacy building: Think about the long-term growth and legacy you want to build, and use 1031 exchanges to help achieve that vision

By executing strategic 1031 exchanges, you can:

- Increase your portfolio's value and diversity.
- Enhance your investment returns.
- Build a lasting legacy.

Keep planning for long-term success!

LONG-GAME LOGAN

Your long-term focus makes 1031 exchanges a natural fit. Here's how to leverage them.

- Target low-maintenance properties: Focus on replacement properties with minimal ongoing management needs, such as professionally managed commercial properties or newer multifamily buildings

- Prioritize stable appreciation: Look for properties with stable, long-term appreciation potential, reducing the risk of market fluctuations
- Build a team of experts: Delegate the exchange process to a team of qualified intermediaries and tax professionals, ensuring everything is done correctly and within the legal framework
- Maintain a balanced lifestyle: Use 1031 exchanges to prioritize passive income opportunities, maintaining a balanced lifestyle while growing your portfolio

By incorporating 1031 exchanges into your strategy, you'll:

- Enhance your long-term stability and security.
- Increase your passive income streams.
- Maintain a balanced lifestyle while growing your wealth.

Keep playing the long game!

Conclusion to Part 4

If there's one thing I hope you take away from this section, it's that you don't have to follow anyone else's playbook to succeed in real estate. I've sold properties in perfect condition and ones that needed work. I've walked away from deals that didn't serve me anymore and leaned into ones that pushed me to grow. And through it all, I've learned that the exit is just as important—if not more—than the entry.

Selling a property isn't giving up on it; it's evolving. It's letting go of what was to make space for what could be. Whether you're off-loading a rental that no longer fits your lifestyle, freeing up capital for a new opportunity, or finally cashing in on years of appreciation, your exit strategy is more than just a line on a spreadsheet; it's a reflection of your goals, your values, and your vision for the future.

So as you evaluate your next move, don't be afraid to think creatively. Trust your gut. Trust your numbers. And most importantly, trust that your journey doesn't have to look like anyone else's. That's the beauty of real estate: You get to write your own ending.

Before you dash off to conquer your next big deal, hold up—I've got a few parting gems for you! Stick around for some final takeaways, a few more personal stories, and a dose of inspiration to keep your real estate journey fired up and moving forward.

Choose Your Hard

We've all heard it—"hard work pays off." And yeah, that's absolutely true. But in real estate investing, there's a twist: It's not just about working hard; it's about *choosing your hard*. The more effort and intention you put into a deal, the bigger the potential payoff. Sounds simple, right? But here's the catch: Where do you draw the line?

Yes, the returns often scale with your hustle—but real estate isn't just a grind. It's also a playground for creativity, problem-solving, and strategic thinking. When you learn to work smart, stay adaptable, and get a little inventive, doors start flying open.

Investing in real estate can be tough—but it's also one of the most flexible, entrepreneurial paths out there, with the power to build serious wealth if you're willing to lean in.

Play to Your Strengths: Leverage Your Unique Skills in Real Estate Investing

It's natural to want to take on every role, especially when starting out. In fact, wearing multiple hats can be beneficial, as it allows you to discover your strengths and weaknesses and identify tasks that are best delegated to others. As your investments grow and you start to scale, it's crucial to learn to delegate effectively. This allows you to focus on high-leverage activities, free up time, and build a sustainable business model.

Understanding your strengths as an investor involves identifying the resources you can contribute to your portfolio, such as:

- **Time:** How many hours can you dedicate to managing properties, finding deals, or handling renovations?
- **Money:** What is your available capital for investments, and what is your access to financing?
- **Skills:** What expertise do you bring to the table, such as construction knowledge, property management experience, or interior design?
- **Network:** Who do you know who can help you find deals, provide financing, or offer valuable advice?

Recognizing your strengths and resources is key to building a successful investment portfolio. By understanding your advantages, you can focus on investments that play to your strengths, outsourcing or partnering on tasks that fall outside your expertise. This intentional approach enables you to build a portfolio that aligns with your goals and capabilities, setting you up for long-term success.

When I first started researching real estate investing, everyone advised me to find my own deals directly from sellers. I took this advice to heart and sent out 1,500 letters to potential sellers, but the responses I received left me baffled. As a new investor with no experience, I quickly realized that finding off-market properties wasn't my strength. Instead, I focused on networking with like-minded individuals, such as real estate brokers, wholesalers, and other investors. This shift in strategy proved instrumental to my success, allowing me to access lucrative deals with significant margins. By shifting the way I looked for deals, I was able to unlock a network of knowledgeable professionals and secure opportunities that I wouldn't have found otherwise.

In addition to understanding your own strengths, it is also important to understand the strengths and weaknesses of the market you are investing in.

Understanding the strengths of your market involves recognizing the unique characteristics, trends, and opportunities present in your local, national, or economic environment. This knowledge enables you to identify emerging trends, capitalize on demand and supply imbalances, and develop targeted investment strategies.

Some key factors to consider when understanding your market's strengths include:

- Consider local economic and demographic drivers like industry growth, job market, population growth, age, and income levels. My favorite site to get this data is the U.S. Census Bureau.
- Look at real estate market conditions like supply and demand, pricing, rental yields. I like using Redfin, Zillow, and the MLS to track trends.
- Dissect national and global economic influences like interest rates, trade policies, and market sentiment. Federal Reserve Economic Data (FRED), Bloomberg, and Trading Economics are all great resources.

When you truly understand what makes your market tick, you can target investments that ride the wave of local demand and long-term growth. For example, if your area is seeing a boom in job growth, that's a golden signal—it could mean demand for housing near employment hubs, office space for expanding companies, or even retail and service businesses to support a growing workforce.

If your market is a college town, student housing or STRs might be the sweet spot. In a city experiencing a surge in tourism? Think boutique hotels, vacation rentals, or entertainment venues. A region with aging demographics? Consider senior housing, medical office space, or wellness centers.

Tapping into these trends means you're not just investing; you're strategically positioning yourself where demand already exists, making your moves smarter, safer, and far more profitable.

Diversifying your portfolio is another key benefit of understanding your market's strengths. By spreading investments across different asset classes, such as residential, commercial, and industrial properties, you can reduce your reliance on a single market segment. Investing in properties with varying risk profiles, such as stable cash-flowing assets versus potential high-growth opportunities, can also help minimize risk and maximize returns. Furthermore, consider diversifying across different geographic areas within your market to minimize exposure to local economic fluctuations.

Staying ahead of the competition requires adapting to changing market conditions. In order to stay on top of this, you need to be continuously monitoring market trends, regulatory changes, and shifts in local demand. By adjusting your investment strategy to respond to changes in the market, you can make the most of new opportunities and mitigate potential risks. For example, you might adapt to new zoning laws or capitalize on emerging industries (like health care or coworking spaces). Staying informed about local development projects, infrastructure plans, and community initiatives can also help you anticipate potential opportunities or challenges.

Ultimately, understanding your market's strengths enables you to make informed decisions that drive long-term success in your investments. You can minimize risk and maximize returns by using data and market analysis to inform investment decisions rather than relying on intuition or emotions. Also, consider seeking advice from local experts, such as real estate agents, attorneys, or financial advisors, to gain valuable insights and guidance into the market that you may not notice yourself.

I am constantly analyzing my own market and diversifying to maintain a steady cash flow while also buying real estate and growing my portfolio. This is a job that is never done, even when you've got a portfolio full of income-generating properties. Those who rest on their real estate laurels often miss out on the next best thing.

Seattle is a prime example of a city with exceptional appreciation potential. With steady growth, a stable job market, and reliable renters, it's an attractive location for long-term investments. However, for those seeking immediate cash flow, Seattle is one of the toughest markets to crack into, due to its high property prices. Additionally, the city's stringent landlord–tenant laws, which favor renters, can further erode cash flow and cause potential challenges with evictions and squatters. While short-term returns may be modest, Seattle's real estate market has consistently demonstrated remarkable long-term growth, with home prices often doubling every seven to ten years, and sometimes even tripling.

Think Outside the Box: Creativity Can Overcome Hurdles in Real Estate

Being creative and thinking outside the box can be a major differentiator in the real estate industry. It's about having a keen eye for spotting hidden gems and untapped potential and being willing to put in the hard work to uncover them.

Additionally, it is important to remember that this industry is full of inevitable curveballs. Whether it's interest rate fluctuations, capital constraints, or intense competition, a strong network can provide valuable insights, creative solutions, and potential partnerships to help overcome these obstacles.

Let's look at a few hurdles you might be currently facing and run through how to overcome them.

Interest rates are high. Consider refinancing or restructuring debt to reduce monthly payments and reduce leverage to minimize risk. Focus on cash-flowing assets, such as rental properties with stable tenants, and diversify your portfolio across different asset classes.

In our current interest rate environment (spring 2025), I'm only looking for seller-financed deals to add to my portfolio, as this will allow me to buy at a lower interest rate with better terms. Seller financing can also provide more flexibility in negotiations, potentially leading to better purchase prices or other benefits. By being selective and targeting these types of deals, you can continue to grow your portfolio while minimizing the risks associated with high interest rates.

There's too much competition in your market. If that's the case, then I recommend that you look for value where no one else is looking. Here are some ways to find value in overlooked areas.

- Explore secondary or tertiary markets—for example smaller cities or towns outside more popular areas
- Find unique property types—like nontraditional properties such as mobile home parks, self-storage facilities, or industrial buildings
- Distressed or neglected properties (these are what I'm always drawn to!)—properties that need renovation or have been neglected but have potential for redevelopment
- Off-market properties—network with local owners, attorneys, or other professionals to find properties not listed publicly

You're short on capital. It is almost impossible to scale without having the funds to invest in deals. If you find yourself in this situation, I advise you to partner with investors, syndicate deals, improve cash flow on your existing portfolio, or do a cash out refinance if you have untapped equity.

There's not enough time to get everything done. Time is a precious commodity, especially for part-time investors juggling a full-time W-2 job. Insufficient time dedication can lead to poor property management, missed opportunities, and inadequate due diligence, which can increase the risk of costly mistakes. To overcome this hurdle, consider outsourcing tasks to professionals (e.g., property management, accounting), focus on one specific strategy, set clear priorities, and, most importantly, delegate tasks to partners or team members where possible.

The birth of my second child marked a turning point in my investment strategy. With time becoming a scarce resource, I was forced to rethink my approach. I shifted from pursuing multiple deals with modest profits to focusing on fewer, high-yield opportunities. This new strategy led me to reject most deals. The year after baby number two was born, instead of acquiring eight to ten properties, I only invested in two. The results were remarkable: I earned a six-figure profit on both deals. This experience transformed the way I approach deal finding, and I'm grateful for the time constraint that prompted me to adapt. (Plus, I love my kid . . . so it all worked out!)

As I reflect on my journey, I've come to realize that knowing when to pivot is just as important as knowing how to push forward. It's a delicate balance between persistence and adaptability, and it's a skill that's essential for success in any field.

Sometimes, the best way to move forward is to change direction. Whether it's due to changes in the market, shifts in personal circumstances, or simply a realization that a new approach is needed, being willing to pivot can be the key to unlocking new opportunities and achieving greater success.

The next time you find yourself facing a challenge or a setback, remember that it may be time to pivot. Don't be afraid to reassess your approach, to seek out new advice, or to try a new strategy. By being open to change and willing to adapt, you'll be better equipped to navigate the twists and turns of your own journey and to achieve your goals.

Doing Well by Doing Good: Philanthropy Can Lead to Great Deals

One ordinary email would soon prove to be the catalyst for an extraordinary opportunity. It was from a stranger, asking if I knew anyone interested in buying a fixer-upper in a specific neighborhood. As fate would have it, that neighborhood was *my own*, and the house was just a four-minute drive from my home.

I responded, expressing my personal interest in the property. The sender, a broker, revealed that the house belonged to her niece and held sentimental value. They wanted to sell it off-market, and to the right buyer. I arranged to see the house, and what I found was a true fixer-upper. I remembered walking through the house, taking in the cluttered rooms, the outdated kitchen, and the worn-out roof. But despite its rough condition, I saw potential. I envisioned the possibilities—the renovations, the redesigns, the transformations. And I knew I had to make it happen.

So I crafted a thoughtful offer, one that took into account the seller's needs and concerns. I included a generous finder's fee for the broker, a token of appreciation for bringing me this incredible opportunity.

My goal was to create a win-win solution for everyone involved. After a few days, the seller accepted my offer, and we went under contract.

But here's where the story takes an astonishing turn. My lender requested an appraisal, which revealed that the property's value was a staggering $600,000 above my purchase price. I was blown away—it was the most incredible appraisal result I'd ever seen in my real estate career.

Curious, I asked the broker how she'd found me and why she'd sent this opportunity my way. Her response left me speechless: "I've attended your walk-throughs and been inspired by your community work. I felt blessed to have someone like you in my market."

In that moment, I realized the profound impact of giving back to the community. By hosting walk-throughs and sharing my expertise, I'd unknowingly created a ripple effect of goodwill. This experience taught me that when you focus on doing good, it can come back to you in unexpected, extraordinary ways.

My Story, Your Inspiration: Sharing My Journey to Help Spark Yours

Since I was a little girl, I have had a burning desire to have a meaningful impact and achieve greatness in my own unique way. Whether it was supporting my family financially or empowering others to pursue their dreams, I knew I was destined for something special.

The fear of disappointing my younger self drove me to persevere, constantly striving to find new opportunities, connections, and growth. I've learned that even the smallest actions can yield significant results and that consistent effort can move the needle, bringing me closer to realizing my dreams.

By stepping out of my comfort zone and exploring new paths, I've been fortunate enough to stumble upon countless opportunities that have shaped my career. One of the most surreal moments was when I emceed the largest BiggerPockets conference in Orlando (You can learn more about BPCON by visiting BiggerPockets.com/BPCON). Inspiring and motivating 3,000 people was an experience I'll never forget! The energy in the room was electric, and I felt honored to play a part in it.

Another unforgettable experience was filming a TV show with James Dainard. It was an absolute blast, and I hope the audience enjoys it just as much as I did.

What I cherish most, though, is the opportunity to share my story with vast communities. My journey hasn't been conventional—I didn't grow up with a silver spoon nor did I have extensive construction knowledge. Yet I've achieved extraordinary results, and I want others to know that they can too.

I hope that the biggest takeaway from my book is that success is within reach, regardless of one's background or circumstances. I'm living proof that ordinary people can achieve remarkable things. My hope is that my story will inspire and motivate you to chase your own dreams, just as I have. Investing in real estate is hard! But it is also creative, entrepreneurial, flexible, and it can be a tool for massive wealth-generation. The returns are directly tied to your effort, making it very lucrative if you are willing to put in the work.

As we conclude this journey through the world of creative exit strategies and stacking profits, I hope you've gained a new perspective on how to maximize the value of your existing portfolio. I want you to know that by thinking outside the box and exploring unconventional approaches, you can unlock hidden potential and create wealth-building opportunities that might have otherwise gone untapped.

Remember, the key to success lies not in simply acquiring properties but in creatively optimizing and repositioning them to generate maximum returns. By utilizing strategies like the value-add strategy, seller financing, and a 1031 exchange, you can create a snowball effect that propels your wealth-building efforts forward.

As you implement these strategies and start seeing results, I encourage you to stay curious, keep learning, and continually adapt to the ever-changing landscape of real estate investing. By doing so, you'll be well on your way to achieving financial freedom and building a legacy that will last for generations.

Thank you for joining me on this journey. I wish you all the best on your path to financial freedom and success!

Now what about our characters? I'd like to offer some final advice to each of the investors we've met along the way.

NEW-TO-THE-GAME NOAH

Don't be discouraged by setbacks or unknowns. Keep learning, stay curious, and surround yourself with experienced mentors and peers. Your eagerness to learn and grow will serve you well in your real estate investing journey.

PIVOT PEYTON

Continue to be agile and adaptable but also prioritize building a strong foundation of knowledge and experience. This will help you make informed decisions and navigate unexpected challenges.

ACTIVE ALEX

Maintain your high energy and enthusiasm, but don't forget to balance action with strategic planning. Stay focused on your goals and adjust your approach as needed.

SEASONED-INVESTOR SAM

Continue to leverage your experience and network to stay ahead of the curve. Don't be afraid to adapt and evolve in response to changing market conditions.

LONG-GAME LOGAN

Keep prioritizing long-term stability and growth. Your focus on sustainable wealth-building will serve you well in the years to come.

And to everyone, I offer these final words of wisdom.

- Stay humble and hungry: No matter how much success you achieve, remain humble and eager to learn
- Build a strong network: Surround yourself with like-minded individuals who share your passion for real estate investing
- Stay adaptable and resilient: Be prepared to pivot in response to changing market conditions and unexpected setbacks

- Pass it on: Share your wisdom and lift others as you climb. Share your knowledge and experience with others, and always look for ways to contribute to your community.

By following these principles and staying committed to your goals, you'll be well on your way to achieving success in real estate investing. Thank you for joining me on this journey!

"You don't have to be great to start, but you have to start to be great."
—Zig Ziglar

Acknowledgments

As I sit down to express my heartfelt gratitude, I am overwhelmed with emotion and appreciation for the incredible journey that has brought this book to life. This project would not have been possible without the love and support of so many amazing individuals who have touched my life in profound ways.

To my husband, Vijay, my partner in every sense of the word—thank you for being my rock, my confidant, and my biggest supporter. Your encouragement and love have given me the courage to chase my dreams, no matter how crazy they may seem.

To my precious children, Rohin and Kian—thank you for your patience and understanding when Mama had to prioritize underwriting deals over making dinner (again!). Your smiles and hugs have kept me going on the toughest of days.

To Mom, Dad, Liki, and Nik—thank you for being my safe haven and my biggest cheerleaders. Our daily Facetime calls have been my lifeline, and I couldn't have navigated the ups and downs of entrepreneurship without you.

To my incredible mentors, James Dainard and Charles McKinney—thank you for believing in me; for sharing your wisdom, expertise, and time; and for pushing me to grow beyond my limits. Your impact on my life and business has been immeasurable.

To the amazing BiggerPockets publishing team—Katie, Kaylee, Savannah, and Winsome—thank you for trusting me with this project, for your tireless efforts, and for your patience. You believed in me when I didn't.

To Amanda, my brilliant editor—thank you for bringing my words to life. You have been an absolute joy to work with, and I couldn't have completed this book without you.

And to my mother, whose love, guidance, and wisdom have shaped me into the person I am today—thank you for being my shining star, my guiding light, and my constant source of inspiration. Your quote, which appears in these pages, is a reminder of the values and principles that have driven me to pursue my dreams.

This book is a testament to the power of collaboration, support, and community. I am humbled by the experience and grateful for the opportunity to share my knowledge and passion with you, the reader. Thank you for joining me on this journey!

About the Author

Leka is a real estate developer and broker based in Seattle, Washington. She is the president of Rehabit Homes, Inc., a company focused on residential and commercial redevelopment. Leka has spearheaded hundreds of transactions, totaling over $100 million in real estate development.

With nearly a decade of experience in repositioning distressed assets, Leka brings a unique blend of vision, strategy, and execution to every project she undertakes. Her expertise lies in revitalizing properties, breathing new life into communities, and creating lasting value.

Beyond her achievements in the real estate industry, Leka is a sought-after speaker. She has emceed prominent conferences such as BiggerPockets and the Best Ever Conference and has also been featured on numerous podcasts and other media, including Business Insider and Fox News. Committed to giving back to her community, she hosts the popular networking mixer "Real Estate at Work," bringing together industry leaders and aspiring professionals to foster connections and knowledge sharing.

Leka moved to the U.S. from India eighteen years ago and has since built a remarkable life and career, exemplifying the American dream. Through her work and philanthropic efforts, Leka continues to inspire and empower others, leaving a lasting legacy in the world of real estate and beyond.

Reference List

"Average Airbnb Occupancy Rates by City [2023]." AllTheRooms. Accessed April 22, 2025. https://www.alltherooms.com/resources/articles/average-airbnb-occupancy-rates-by-city/.

Britton, David. "Short-Term Rentals Real Estate Statistics: Will the Market Thrive?" DoorLoop. January 9, 2025. https://www.doorloop.com/blog/short-term-rentals-real estate-statistics#:~:text=this%20booming%20market.-,By%20the%20year%202026%2C%20the%20short%2Dterm%20rental%20market%20is,19.1%25%20from%202022%2-0to%202032.

Kiyosaki, Robert. *Rich Dad Poor Dad*. Plata Publishing, 1997.

Lane, Jamie. "Airbnb Occupancy Rate: Highs, Lows, & Calculating Your Own." AirDNA. March 10, 2024. https://www.airdna.co/blog/airbnb-hosting-tips-for-occupancy-in-2023.

Reed, Catherine. "35 Insightful Landlord Statistics – 2023." Flex. January 9, 2023. https://getflex.com/blog/landlord-statistics.

Richardson, Nela. "The Age of Work." ADP Research. January 27, 2025. https://www.adpresearch.com/the-age-of-work/.

SUPERCHARGE YOUR REAL ESTATE INVESTING.

Get **exclusive bonus content** like checklists, contracts, interviews, and more when you buy from the BiggerPockets Bookstore.

Use code **FirstBPBook** for **15%** off your first purchase.

Standard shipping is free and you get bonus content with every order!

www.BiggerPockets.com/STORE

BiggerPockets Newsletter Signup

Want access to more content? Sign up for the BiggerPockets Newsletter using the QR Code below. Covering a range of current topics of conversation, keep in the know about investing in your area.

Sign up now:
www.BiggerPockets.com/newsletter

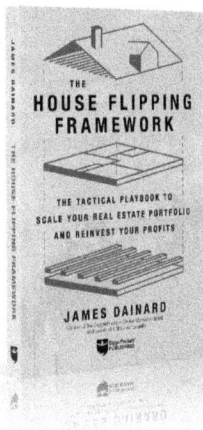

The House Flipping Framework: The Tactical Playbook to Scale Your Real Estate Portfolio and Reinvest Your Profits

By James Dainard

Acomprehensive guide to efficiently flipping properties and maximizing profits from expert house flipper James Dainard.

BiggerPockets.com/ReadFlippingFramework

The Small and Mighty Real Estate Investor: How to Reach Financial Freedom with Fewer Rental Properties

By Chad Carson

Rather than chasing a goalpost that always moves, a small and mighty investor keeps their strategy simple to maximize flexibility and build the life they want.

BiggerPockets.com/ReadSmallandMighty

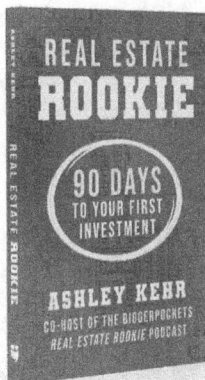

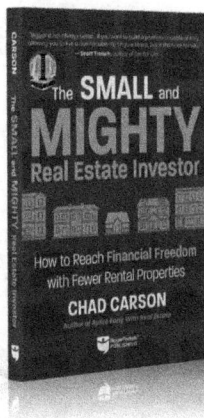

Real Estate Rookie: 90 Days to Your First Investment

By Ashley Kehr

Ashley has helped thousands achieve real estate success, including listeners of the BiggerPockets *Real Estate Rookie* podcast and attendees of the Real Estate Rookie Bootcamp.

BiggerPockets.com/ReadRookie

Looking for more?
Join the BiggerPockets Community

BiggerPockets brings together education, tools, and a community of more than 3 million+ like-minded members—all in one place. Learn about investment strategies, analyze properties, connect with investor-friendly agents, and more.

Go to **BiggerPockets.com** to learn more!

Listen to a **BiggerPockets Podcast**

Watch **BiggerPockets on YouTube**

Join the **Community Forum**

Learn more on **the Blog**

Read more **BiggerPockets Books**

Learn about our **Real Estate Investing Bootcamps**

Connect with an **Investor-Friendly Real Estate Agent**

Go Pro! Start, scale, and manage your portfolio with your **Pro Membership**

Follow us on social media!

Join over 3 million investors on BiggerPockets forums. Whether you're a seasoned expert or just starting out, tap into the collective knowledge, confidence, and connections to reach your full potential.

Join the conversation now!

BiggerPockets.com/BookForums

BiggerPockets®

www.ingramcontent.com/pod-product-compliance
Lightning Source LLC
Jackson TN
JSHW080816110825
88905JS00002B/2